About My Cat and Other Tales

About My Cat
and Other Tales

written and illustrated by
Brian J. Fournier

Haley's

Athol, Massachusetts

Haley's
488 South Main Street
Athol, MA 01331
marcia2gagliardi@gmail.com
978.249.9400

Illustrations by Brian J. Fournier.
Cover illustration by Brian J. Fournier.

Proof read by Richard Bruno.

Library of Congress Cataloging-in-Publication Data
Names: Fournier, Brian J., 1948- author, illustrator.
Title: About my cat : and other tales / written and illustrated by Brian J.
    Fournier.
Other titles: About my cat (Compilation)
Description: Athol, Massachusetts : Haley's, [2023] | Summary: "Verse and
    illustrations both lighthearted and thoughtful"-- Provided by publisher.

    Identifiers: LCCN 2022026964 (print) | LCCN 2022026965 (ebook) | ISBN
    9781948380645 (paperback) | ISBN 9781948380652 (pdf)
    Subjects: LCGFT: Poetry.
    Classification: LCC PS3606.O8444 A64 2023 (print) | LCC PS3606.O8444
    (ebook) | DDC 811/.6--dc23/eng/20220610
    LC record available at https://lccn.loc.gov/2022026964
    LC ebook record available at https://lccn.loc.gov/2022026965

for my wife, Marlene Chaisson,
who helped me to open up

My world works because of her.
She nurtures me to create.

Contents

The Sweetness of Innocent Intention
Followed by a Gut Punch

a foreword by Candace Anderson

Brian Fournier creates art while writing poetry in no less than what he identifies as an act of survival. He shares his evocative art and poetry in *About My Cat and Other Tales*. Survival requires sharp personal insights as well as astute assessments of one's surroundings. With compelling pen and ink drawings along with poetry deeply personal and sometimes edgy, Fournier clearly reveals both skills.

Creative endeavors often seem profound when they consider universal constructs by exploring personal truths. Fournier invites his readers to glimpse the inner world of his personal truths — innocence, creativity, and sensitivity. Yet, he doesn't flinch from sharing painful truths about his life within the constructs of the outer world.

His act of sharing is bold — an elegant contrast to the finesse of the drawings in pen and ink. Fournier adeptly uses fine lines and pointillism to illustrate portraits and poses of his dear cat along with other subjects prominent in the artist's evolving life. At times, the drawings are so fine they nearly seem to dissolve into the cosmos they inhabit on the picture plane. Many of the drawings find their power through such delicacy, a perfect foil for the emotional force of the story revealed through Fournier's poetic voice.

Fournier's poetry comes alive in complex underpinnings that emerge in sharing of a simple moment, such as a communication with his cat. The gentle tone rewards the reader with the sweetness of innocent intention followed by a gut punch of acute pain from an abrupt act that annihilates the sweetness.

The poems sweep broadly through autobiographical childhood episodes and into the angst and challenges of Fournier's transformative adult persona. Through it all, Fournier never wavers from speaking his truth with a genuine and skillful voice.

Fournier wisely assesses creativity as an act of survival. The pretense of seeking accolades never drives his creative motivation. Fournier focuses on the rich process of seeing and interpreting the world—his personal world as well as the outer world shared by the reader. The resulting splendid book touches upon what it is to be human.

And the feline companion seems to intuit many of the answers.

Retired educator Candace Anderson of Petersham, Massachusetts, is a Signature Member of New England Watercolor Society.

Explanation with Thanks

a preface by Brian J. Fournier

My work here is about surviving the world in my lifetime. I use poems to express myself and right my ship, so to speak. I've spent the past fifty-plus years putting the poems on paper. My brothers and I share many memories. Even though I'm the youngest, some of my memories are somewhat foggy, so I've filled them with my impressions.

Poems about my cat, real or not, represent my conversations with her, and I stand by them. Perhaps you also dabble in other languages. I am quite fluent—or at least I was—with my cat.

I just like to say that, as each day comes and goes, I feel like I uncover more of myself buried many years ago in the authoritarian climate of my childhood. A so-sensitive child never had a chance at art and was not nurtured in that direction. So with each day, I find more and more of my artistic nature. I perform art by writing, mastering many forms of drawing and painting, and playing and creating music. They are the acts I find I need to survive.

The soundest reason for the poems is my wife, Marlene. My thirty-plus years with her have seen me grow so much, and I attribute that growth to the atmosphere I live in. She is very wise, patient, and strong and accepts me completely. My successes have come to fruition because of my wife. She was the one who helped me to open up. My trust in her was all I needed. She became my muse, my biggest fan, my most discerning critic, and my manager. If I had her energy and dedication, I could have produced a hundred books and a thousand pieces of art by now. My world works because of her. She nurtures me to create.

Ideas are sacred. Embrace them!

Developing My Secret Side

an introduction by Brian J. Fournier

I've heard it said that writers are born, not made. I believe that is true. I would add that it is true for all types of artists. With me it was true as far back as I can remember. Something about me was different. I was different from my brothers, my friends, from everyone I met. I had a secret side to me, and I wouldn't show it to anyone. That persona would develop for decades.

I was shy and, I'd say with great certainty, I was a wallflower in school. My childhood made me withdrawn. Stephen King once explained that, when he writes, it's like he is an archeologist digging and brushing away the sands until he unearths the entire story. I'd say my life has been like that. I grew up with a very unpredictable parent who could be very harsh and mean. He brought fear into my life, and fear is a paralyzing by-product of violence that can ruin a person's confidence and self-reliance. It took me many years to forge my way through that stigma and emerge from a life based on avoiding fear.

Here is a quick story about my fear. When I was fourteen, and the Beatles came out big in the United States, it was all I needed to push myself into taking guitar lessons. I always loved music and spent most days of my life listening and singing alone in the house or where no one could hear me. So I bought a guitar and set up music lessons across town. I had to walk across town with my guitar. For me, it was too much after one lesson. I decided I was too dumb to learn. After all, my father had told me for fourteen years how stupid I was—I think I believed him. Also, I was too shy to walk down the street with my guitar in hand. When I think about it today, I'm floored. The me of today would strut down the street giving it everything to succeed. I have since taught myself to play the guitar. But that example shows how a person can let fear stop them from succeeding no matter how much they want something.

When you live that way, creating is impossible. But when you keep it to yourself, there are no negatives. Years later, I managed to produce quite a bit of work for my secret side. I did not *want* to create. It was a necessary need: I *had* to create. Inside of me, creation was a fever punching its way out. It took me many years to dare show anyone my work. Once I did, I could not stop and was encouraged by my family to produce more and more. So I started adding more areas in my desire to create and express.

With me, expression comes as self need. When I go to art shows and people see my work and praise me, it is a great feeling. Some will say, "Wow! You're really good!" or "Beautiful work!" I like hearing those kudos, but they don't mean as much to me as the feeling I get during the creation of the art. I live for the expression.

Sometimes with the euphoria of creating comes the frustration of believing you missed the mark. You didn't match what's on paper with what you had in your head. You end up feeling the failure and not the euphoria. That comes with the territory. Creation cuts both ways. So you go to bed at night, and tomorrow is a new day—get up and go at it again. It can be a grind or a magical manifestation, both in writing and drawing.

The difficulty with creating is knowing when something is done. Our teacher from Master Class Creative Writing told us about a famous writer who said, "A writer doesn't ever finish a book, they give up on it." In other words, get the work to the apex, and when you can't make it better, give up. I'm not sure that works in writing, and I know it doesn't work in drawing or painting, because in artwork you can overwork and ruin a piece quite easily. I think you can do that in writing, too. The catch is to always have that template in your head to match to the finished product. No match, no win! If you get close and can't do any better, be satisfied or tear it to pieces (confetti sometimes) and start again.

My poems are about what my secret side has been noticing for many years. The sketches to go along with each poem are images that come to my mind with each poem. The drawings are all freehand. The drawings convey my idea of the poem, not necessarily the reader's idea.

I've studied poetry and writing for many years, and my philosophy on poetry resides in the non-elitist realm. I come from the Wordsworth camp. Furthermore, I believe that you should not need a PhD to understand a poem. To paraphrase William Carlos Williams, poetry should come from simple things, the things that you stumble over every day.

Since poems use similes and metaphors, I believe they should have an understandable design. Robert Frost defined those figures of speech as "*saying something and meaning something else.*" Also, poets use words that could mean more than one thing or are vague just as Shakespeare wrote five hundred years ago in his Sonnet 18: "so long lives *this* and *this* gives life to thee." The *this* he refers to is the poem. The idea he disguises is that the poem lives so the *thee* lives every time someone reads it. I read it, and *thee* just lived again.

One other point I want to make is that I love rhyme and meter. Today, there is much free verse that I like as well. Some subjects work better as free verse. But to structure a poem and have it rhyme well without sacrificing content and to have the meter consistent so that it flows present quite a challenge. I enjoy that challenge at times. And I like to read structured poetry.

The Poet

The Poet

Some days to dream,
other days reflect,
gathering cream
for a moment's respect—

astride an eon,
an image in time,
one wandering pawn
in search of a rhyme.

—1984

Mind to Mind

Mind to Mind

"People are crazy," I heard her say.
"What makes you think that?" I asked.
She blinked at me as if I should know,
her tail curled around her feet,
It was before we sent her away.
"Because we're in control?" I answered myself.
No response, just a blink,
then she looked away.
Was I imagining again?
Imagining we were speaking?
Believing her wisdom again?
"Are you?" She questioned.
Her green eyes read my mind.
"Of course, we are," I blurted nervously.
I swear I saw her smile.
Her thin lips exposed teeth.
She looked at me and away, then back again,

So, that's it. We were conversing mind to mind!

"Only one question," she asked using telepathy.
I waited, looked at her and waited.
It was a long time we stared
back and forth.
"WHAT??" I finally howled, startling her.
She jumped down and walked away,
but I heard the question
fall over her slinky shoulders,
"Is that what makes you human?"
                                        —2002

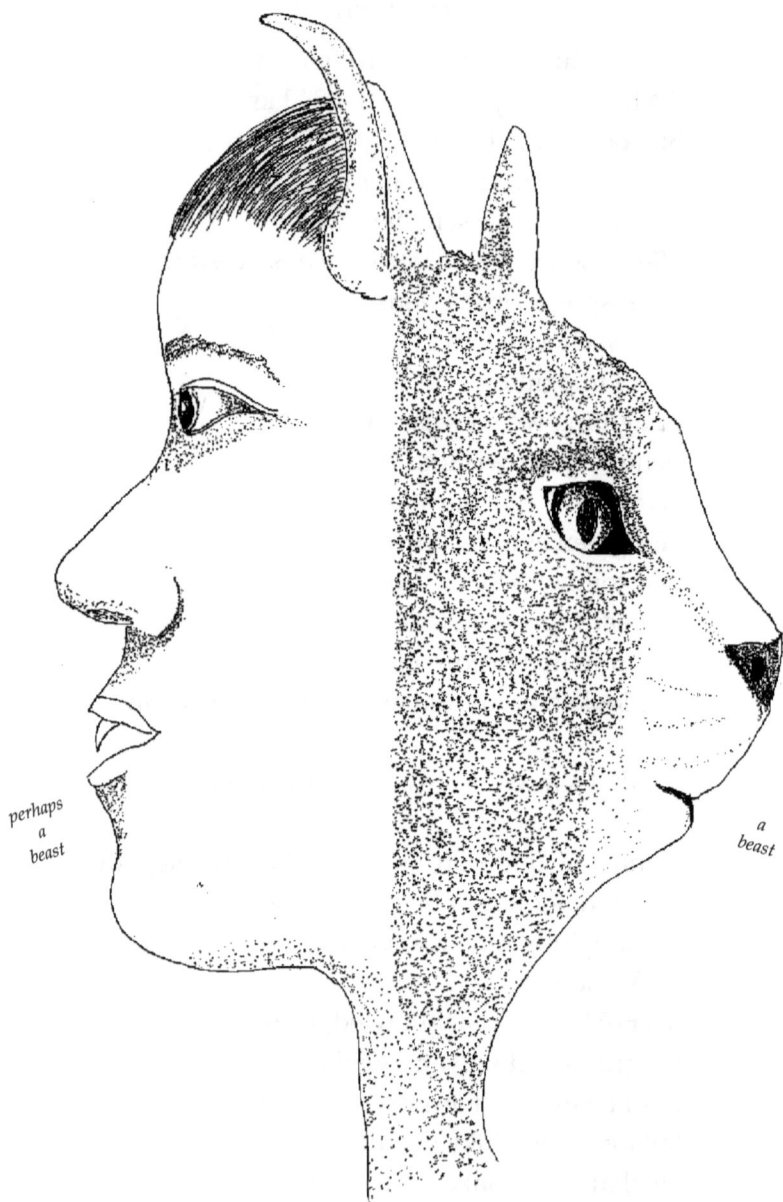

perhaps
a
beast

a
beast

About My Cat

About My Cat

The woods-boy he once was
darted out of that place
wary of ruling hands
like a mouse from a hawk.

She called him "a beast."
"All men are beasts!" she said.
He wished it were so
instead of being human.

What are shadows other than
light my cat would avoid?
She was ardent for carpet
square spots of skylight sun
so simple and graceful
worthy of being a beast!

Away from her anger,
he mused on manhood.
Was he justified? Or did
he hold to standards required
for being a beast?

—2002

A Little Boat

A Little Boat

There was a little boat
on a shimmering lake,
and, as its sail unfurled,
the wind was just right
that the boat carved a path
through the lapping water
from this inlet to that.
In the act of moving,
the little boat's bow sang
upon the dark waters
as if it were thanking
the gods for some purpose.
Such a contented sound
as the water glistened
silhouettes of sky.
A triangle of canvas
an artist would pat on,
carefully blending smoothly
every hue necessary
for essence on liquid.

But, of course,
the little boat
was not able to thank
the water for friction
or the wind for motion.

But,
if I were a little boat,
I could thank you!

—2012

11

About an Old Poem

About an Old Poem

Found in a stack of magazines —
I felt so much at that moment,
so very much about something
and so little about the words
to cast them away forgotten
between *Writer's Digest* and *Time*.

I wrote so prolifically
about my cat that she believed me
and has herself become a poet
with her paw-pads smudged in ink.

She finds an age to recent art,
a balance reflecting masters
as an associate said then
upon their visit to England,
"It seemed so civilized there."

—1996

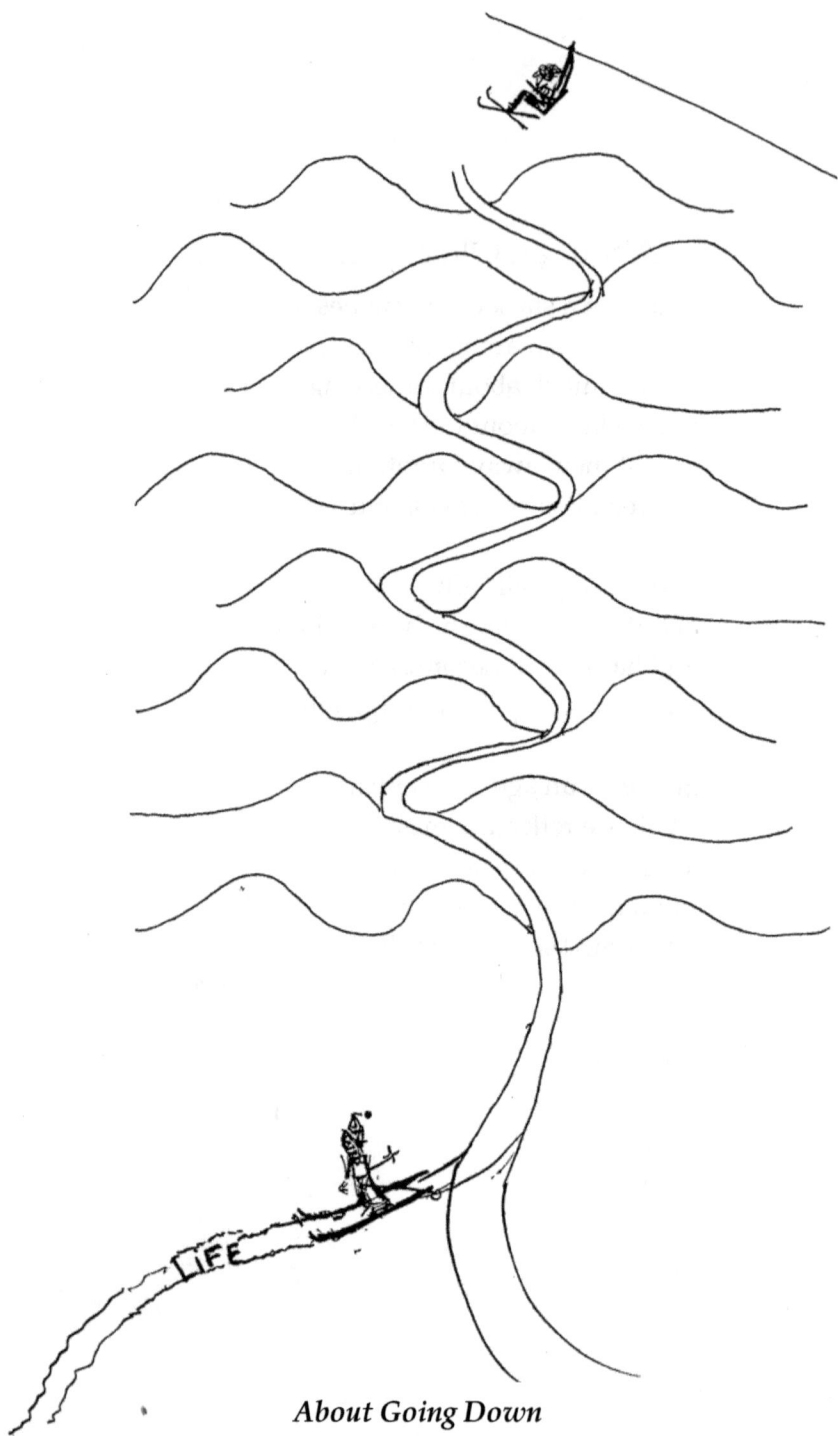

About Going Down

About Going Down

Somewhere on a chairlift, it came to me . . . the meaning of life!
"I understand," I said to him.
"I know what we've been doing wrong. You have to go . . . "
"Straight down," he said, finishing my sentence.
"Yes!" I said. "Straight down."
"You don't turn at all. You go straight. You don't turn.
You gotta go straight down. Let the moguls hit you. Absorb them.
They turn your skis. They don't change your course."
"How do you control your speed?"
he asked as we slid from lift to hill.
"You don't," I answered. "That's the key! You gotta

Go

Straight

Down

You . . .

Can't . . .

Worry . . .

About . . .

Speed . . . "

. . .

—1995

15

The Mending Wall
The Vietnam Memorial

The Mending Wall • The Vietnam Memorial

"Something there is that doesn't love a wall"
— Robert Frost

Winter sky frowned small concerns of doubt
as his poem steamed upon the air
spoken with a nod and shake that
stilled my crunching steps
perhaps earth overlaps and the edge
is black and smooth, plowed
for some forgotten ground.

The prayer tugged at his quivering lips
an outstretched hand joined the stone
crimson in the cold like
a rose on a tomb.

Seemingly it immersed granite like a swan
dipping into a lake reflection
this reservoir was frozen
and his audible objections
echoed
endlessly
on
stone.

I stood within a man's silent honor.

A voice droned priest-like vespers across a mere —
blue fingertips wedged on a name
as ivory rain weighed on his
withering form.

Then I caught a reflection, a uniformed soul . . .

Water distorts, but I saw him reaching for the hand
the rose upon a name — the name
holding him there . . .

I would have helped him, too, but
I was reaching for my own.

—1992

17

Dance

Dance

As every weekday I sat at my desk
quite contented in that desk chair
dreaming dreams with the best —
With coffee's warmth in my stare —

And as I worked just after dawn,
the business world began to yawn.
Around me some start to chatter.
Papers shuffled. Typewriters clattered.

The volume rose with the sun
bringing life where there was none.
My office has no walls to know.
It's open to such busy flow.

I could feel the moving air
like the heat and cold we shared
as every cheery face appeared.
Each star twinkled as it neared.

Smiling people groomed with care
bound with duty they must share.
Now the hum has reached a pitch
like someone finally pulled the switch.

So like a dance, the music's begun,
And I may choose to dance this one.

—1978

Another Day to Save

Another Day to Save

A distant reflection
touches an ocean
sinking the sun
beneath a wave.
A hollow horizon
swallows a promise
ending devotion
winds take away.

Now, a darkening
provocation hopes for
another day to save!

—1977

Another Spring

Another Spring

*written on the occasion of
my father's death*

Looking out the window,
hardly mentioning my name,
such indifference in his stare —
they were sad eyes just the same.
Perhaps they found forgiveness
with the edge of some regret,
but they were looking somewhere,
and they could not forget.

Were they waiting eyes,
contemplating what must turn?
Surely they were preoccupied
with whatever they must learn.
I spoke to them directly,
their waver was but slight
and left me for some vision
yet answered me in spite,
"I'd like to see another spring."
His voice had changed in size,
allowing me just a glimpse
beyond those searching eyes.

Somehow I think my dad knew
his last wish would remain
sealed among those lost hopes
I continue to disdain.

—1988

23

Anxiety Is Purple

Anxiety Is *Purple*

I bought a hand squeezer from China —
well, not directly from China, but it
had the word CHINA embossed on its
rubber casing like a strange growth
on the skin of a very purple plum.
Some Asian laborer must have taken
a rubber sack and filled it with a
combination of hair gel and ball bearings,
then cauterized the sack opening closed —
STRESS BALL, the carton read in caps.
At times, I squeezed it readily
to see the word **CHINA** bulge to
a number twenty-four font.

One day, a cohort said about me,
he's going to squeeze that Stress Ball
in his hour of need, and the entire load
of ball bearings will explode from that
sack and roll over the sales floor like
the balls of serotonin scrambling
from his brain. My head feels that way,
an erstwhile cerebration squished, thumping,
and pulsing a purple but audible, cognitive
CHINA **CHINA CHINA**
Like I'll burst at the seams
losing all my ideas as so many
marbles rolling down an endless
flight of stone stairs,
sounding me hollow,
leaving me empty indeed
but for the distant . . .

CHINA CHINA **CHINA CHINA**
— 2003

25

APPOINTMENTS
FRIDAY   30

9 Funeral
10 Gardner
11 Westminster
12 Leominster
1 Lunenburg
2 Fitchburg
3 Erving
4 Orange
5 Athol

ACE
FUNERAL
HOME

Appointments for the Day

Appointments for the Day

I asked for an hour:
it's for her funeral!
"Yes, boss, my appointments
are all set for today!"

So we dropped into
a people-filled church as
a stoic priest mumbled
about our savior Christ.
Not of our dear friend or
how we should cope with loss
and the terms of her life but
the rudiments of sin!

With my mindfulness gone,
I was there daydreaming . . .
those long days in summer
when sun marks our time
and how reflections make
the water more beautiful
like the ripples a stone
makes upon a lone shore.
We remember the wake
and how it bent the water
to its place in our world.

The silence brought me back
to something unfulfilled as
the numbness on my mind
seemed much heavier.

Especially for those
appointments for the day!
I must remember to
cross her off my list . . .

—1997

27

Balancing Life

Balancing Life

Me	Dad
Our summer vacation,	"Goddamn kids!"
the ferns were unfolding.	"Nothing to do!"
Our island south of town	
those stonewalls holding.	
A side of road hugged—	"I'll take those bikes away."
"Truck!" Ron said.	
He shouted, "Stay!"	
steel gears—rubber rolling,	"Jesus Christ!"
dog Susie so far away.	"She should have been tied up."
She doesn't know with which	"You kids shouldn't be riding—
kid she should be staying.	not on the frigging road!"
We're balanced on our side—	
across she was weighing.	"This is your fault!"
Yells seem to confuse her,	
the surface quite sandy.	
She lay there bleeding,	"My best fucking hunting dog!"
her insides like candy.	
With each of us crying,	
Bro Ron took the blame.	"God damn you, Ron,
I'll never forget her.	you stupid son of a bitch."
It won't be the same.	"You're all stupid."

—1995

Death of a Friend

Death of a Friend

Me	**Dad**
Just try not to be looking	
while holding a flashlight	"God damn it! !"
steady	
should you go to a shooting	
on a dark November night.	
Our beagle was pregnant,	Some mutt knocked her up."
and we only asked why:	
just aid as requested	"Hold that light still!"
to witness her die.	
I remember her face,	"HOLD THAT LIGHT STILL
how she met her sad end.	BETWEEN THE EYES."
I held the light steady	"I'll take care of you,
for the death of a Friend.	God damn it!"

—1995

31

Because of Him . . .

Because of Him . . .

July's smothering humidity was a hazy hook
as we rounded the pond, really just a brook.
The valley so sweltered as we tramped
to a spillway's water backed up to a swamp.

At the shore's murkiness, Hunter drank
to escape the heat. To my knees I sank.
Unclasped, a retriever believes in the swim,
but it was fear I weighed as I plunged in.

In spite of my dread, it was Hunter's jones
and Nick Adams's swamp that we would roam.
My shoes squished home like a hollow voice.
I followed Hunter and thought of my choice.

My imagination had me less than brave,
as if how to crawl into some slimy cave.
It was Hunter the bold that led the way —
because of him, I'll never forget that day!

God bless you, Hunter!

—2018

Blood Brothers

Blood Brothers

What really is a hero?
Is it the action of the soul?
Is it thought without cost?
Is it price without worth?
Is it conscientiousness?
Is it boundless humanity?
Or is it a bond for life?
Blood brothers are not twins,
but mine saved me many
times—
fifty-plus years ago
with strong arms carrying me,
head bleeding from a fall
all those steps from home.
Or when he pounded me
to dislodge that bright penny
to end my choking fit.
Or on a roller coaster, when
unable to break his grasp,
my terror leap would fail.

Or when a marriage ended,
he gave me his own home.
Or when shame could win,
he showed me the truth.
Or when my life of crashes
tempted me to seek an end,
he saved me once again.
He taught me survival.

A brother is one you fight.
A brother is one you hate.
A brother is one you love.
A brother is one you know.
But you don't know him well
until you see the hero.
My brother is my hero!
I'd lend him to everyone,
but it takes more to make one
than I ever realized.
It takes a brother's love.

—2017

Cash

Cash

What creatures be
who fell on this Earth
with no set ideas
or wisdom of worth?

Considered themselves
beings of God.
From a garden they fell,
so originally flawed.

Civilized? No!
Instincts will show
they fight and murder
for things and dough.

To exceed wasn't enough.
They just want more,
some sort of lust
to feed their self-whore.

Greed — is it human,
a trait, a multiple rife?
Would they find the true side
of a double-edged knife?

From birth to death,
they never seem aware
that this mortal cash race
will lead to despair.

— 2018

From Where They Came

From Where They Came

Melodies can't help those words.
They will not join a song.
An instrument at its best
can never sound as strong.

No need of catchy beats
portrayed on video—
not in a famous singer
or an awards TV show.

No,

they fall silent like snow
landing somewhere in time
as if a kindly, traveling Joe
delivered his mind-chime.

They join in straight lines.
Orderliness must guide
and never to be shrouded.
Ideas should not hide.

Their cost is almost nothing—
not fortune, success, nor fame—
just the sweat for borrow
as we ask them back again.

Will they ever find their way,
those words inside our brain,
as they travel through their wonderland
to be from where they came?

—1979

Chips May Fall

Chips May Fall

Reason comes so shiny.
Steel chips are curling fine.
Rounded as a revolving door
rolling off one's mind,
they fall upon the floor.

Shaping one's faith numbs
in art's illusive baiting,
not like a sculptor's crumbs
nor the dust he is creating,
but what his vision becomes.

I'm thinking, as these chips
squiggle into wordities,
I'll let them cool like sips
to avoid my past absurdities,
the scars upon my fingertips.

In this pall, I see the smears,
those marks made by recall—
inner wounds expelling fears,
a reason the chips may fall.
They brand you with ideas.

—2009

Cage

Cage

Blown spring trees
whirled like ballerinas,
as if fingers gripped
blue-green designs
as remembrances,
played in a scene ended,
a love story unrequited,
all including the ache —
a quaking weakness
unable to save or rescue
how Nature's giant winds
smashed hope to pieces.
A broken bruised heart!
How sinews of a bitter soul
bled from lost promise.

I said to her, "Despair,"
explaining my silence.
When a whisper returned,
I saw what she saw —
the world outside her cage!

—2003

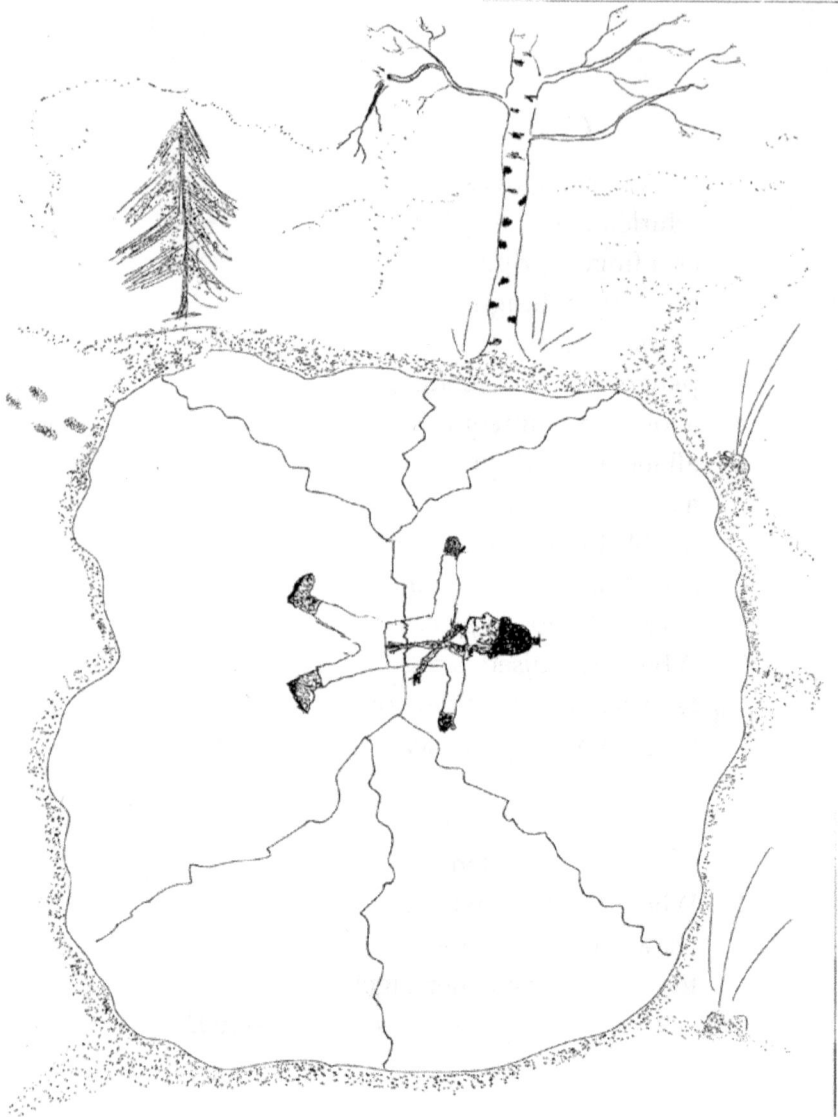

Broken

Broken

I saw them lined up
at a bus stop and was
reminded of those days —
a country road, winter,
many years ago —
a boy running beyond
a field of crusted snow
to a frozen marsh,
a somber red face
reflected from the ice
he'd mittened clean
to expose bubbles
frozen halfway up.
His knees tingled so cold
as he rolled over to watch
a wind move the clouds away.

Earth can nurture the disparaging,
so never judge a boy or
how broken he's become
by those who never dreamed.

—2003

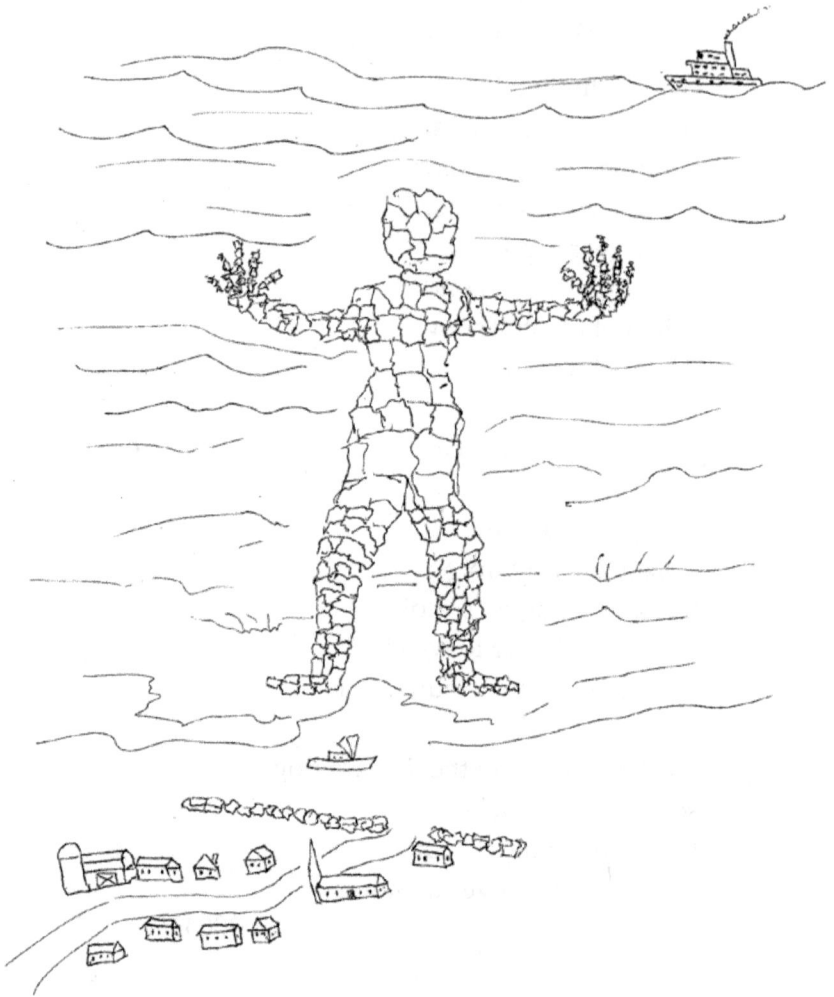

Breakwaters Call

Breakwaters Call

A small swell rises.
A lonely rolling wave
solemnly reprises,
sweeping in its stave,
bent as though profiling
a curl against the cage.
A harbor's granite piling
meets a deafening rage.
It seats the shipless shores
watching a span of ocean
balancing wherefores,
each stone against motion,
depth beyond clarity
focusing the soul,
telling all disparity
to never, ever fold.

Here with feet firmly put,
I stand at breakwater's call
and face each crest foot by foot,
determined not to fall.

—1984

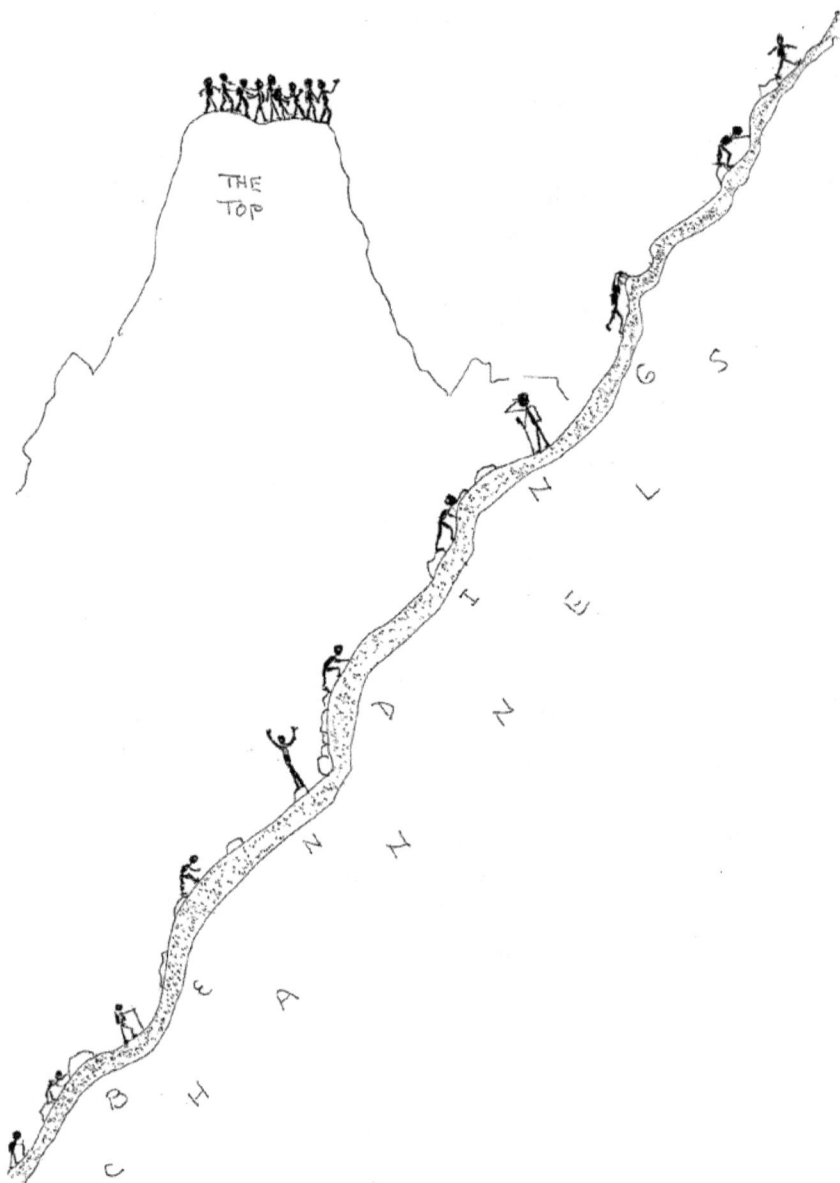

Bending Channels

Bending Channels

Frosted blue morn
bound us in race
as Nature bestowed
a crystalline grace.
With commitment, yet,
we ventured our stride
and followed that path
up a mountainside.
Perhaps to summit
and ride our thrill,
we were liquid running
as if flowing uphill.
As if blood might gush
in veins of Earth,
bending channels
back to birth!
With a thigh-aching climb
at the edge of control,
we took that mountain
to her soul.

—1999

Bad Weather Ahead

Bad Weather Ahead

A buck sprang over a stonewall,
paused a second to study me.
I stood perfectly still, and he
glided off after some moments.

I observed him tracking.
Crunching snow echoed
his effort of pleasure as
he sniffed air and sensed.
Quickly, he took in the
bluish-yellow horizon
as if he could reason
world out of necessity!

I'm sure
instincts told him
bad weather ahead,
find a safe place, and
settle in for the night.

I viewed the same sky,
concluded the same thought:
bad weather ahead!
And with all my reasoning,
I couldn't think of a safe place
to find in this lifetime.

—2008

Bee Dance

Bee Dance

written on the occasion of
my mother's death

I recalled she loved it!
Duty with needs,
it was the gift of self.
It is so with love and bees.

Dancing destination
so her sisters may vie,
dispersing Nature's hope
into the morning sky.

I told them about her —
how the loss had me blue —
so they would not leave
as worried bees do!

Seeing them come and go
on my perch near their hive,
an example bees share.
It's hard work staying alive.

Each one the perfect wife
making spring flowers,
a solitary giver,
on mother's hours.

The average female honey bee lives about thirteen
days,
they work themselves to death for one thing, the hive,
the family. Mothers are bees.

—1993

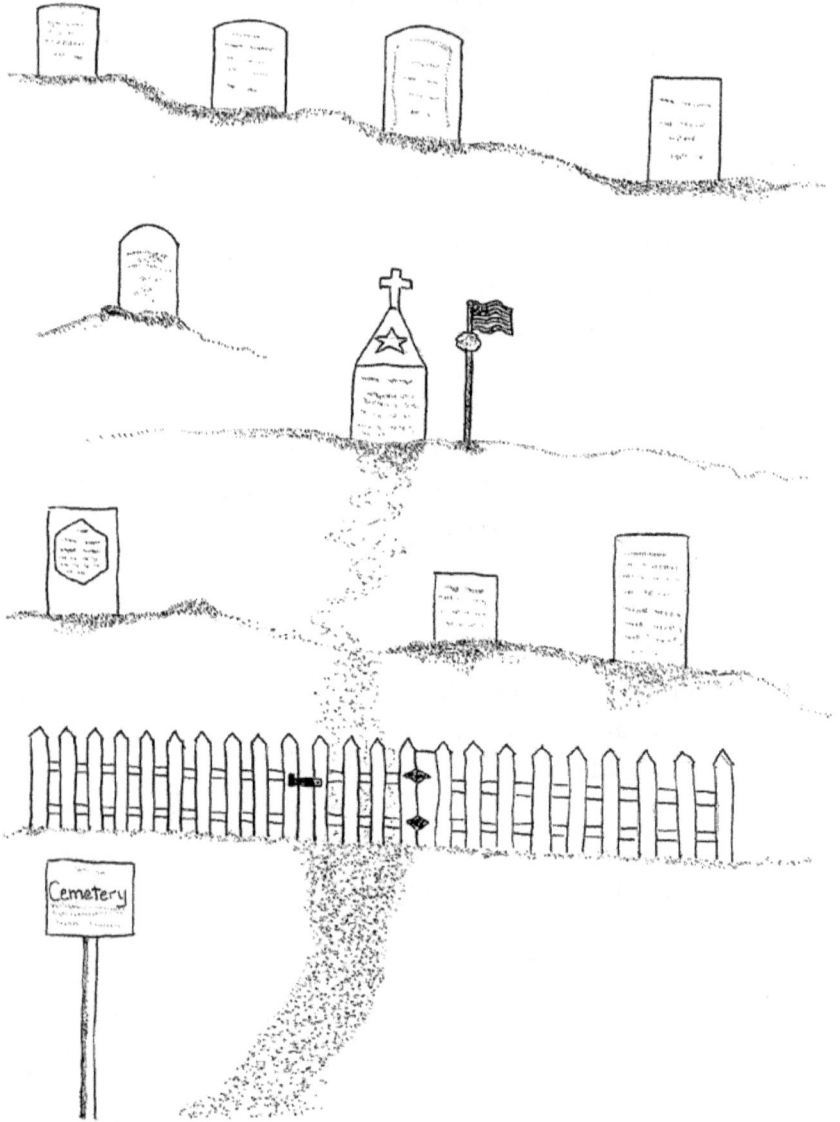

Cemetery

Cemetery

a sonnet

We pass this place as silent strangers do
while dusk arrives to a day aging late.
The flag is folded then by one or two,
and picket-wood slats part, as does our gait.
Enclosed is a hero for every home,
an invisible shape. Distant light has kept
his soul imprisoned with the grounds to roam.
We chase the empty fall of every step.
The forgotten face of time grays with lines,
a memory they once washed yearly,
for over there is where the soldier died
while in here we miss the child so dearly.
Now, with our cadence questioning regret
we pause in dim light, never to forget.

—1985

Suitor to the Sea

Suitor to the Sea

Surely she does call me
as spring brides do in May,
beckons all the summer
when I have been away.

She does not doubt intention
nor question my reprieve,
just rolls her eyeless waves
a restless crashing heave.

Land-locked in my prison:
an airless musky gasp
remembers her fragrance,
our liaisons of past.

Perhaps you know her slightly,
the tactile of her face,
and respect that mighty power
that no man dare disgrace.

For me, I'm ever faithful
despite our time apart.
On moonlit nights I feel her
tugging at my heart.

The most dangerous of lovers
impossible to tame—
those who fall unto her
understand her claim.

It's not so disappointing
to know that I must be—
a courtier to windmills
and suitor to the sea.

—1979

From Swirling Pools

From Swirling Pools

To me it seems
writing looks fine
on yellow paper,
a fountain pen,
an X-fine nib,
moments alive,
as if dying in
liquified puddles
drying black, as
wet lava rocks
lined on a sun
drenched
beach.

Once sages dipped
quill in wells so black
that
diamond words clung
from swirling pools,
solidified lines of
prose and posey
as if mining light
from a sullen night.

I, too, with racing mind
loaded my pen in time
to scratch upon a line
on prize yellow bond,
by design,
and behind
those ideas,
my thoughts
so prepared —
I forgot!

Renewed,
the ink sludge
on my nib had
solidified.

—2016

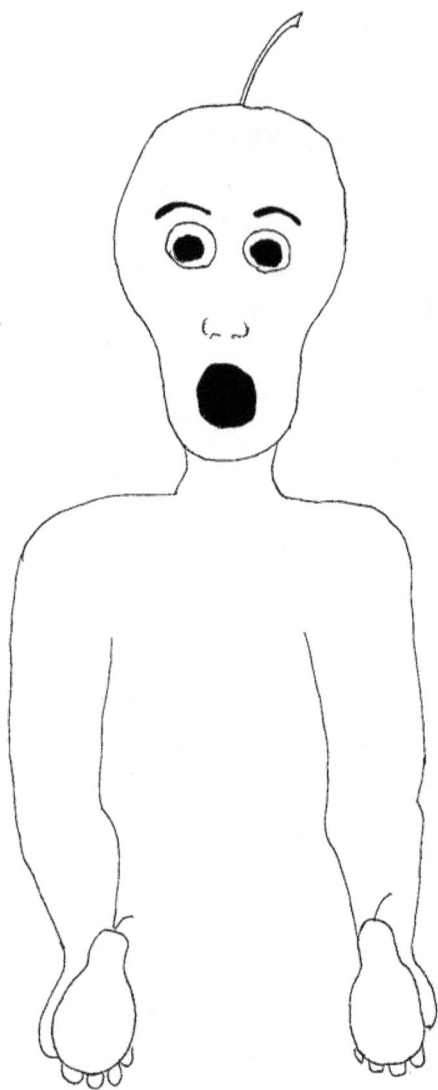

Despair

Despair

You too are rare, it's plain to see.
My delicate pear, disclose this to me.
I can't determine from your hue
if I will sin from taking you.

Oh, pear of mine, I am so confused.
You are divine and nary bruised,
so I can't decide if I dare
take one of you or the pear . . .

          —1980

Disappears

Disappears

Fingers reach from the hand.
There they breach the bleach-white sand
to capture what dreamers do.
The waters wash
as destined to.
A sun grows higher
and ocean nears.
A castle spire disappears . . .

—1984

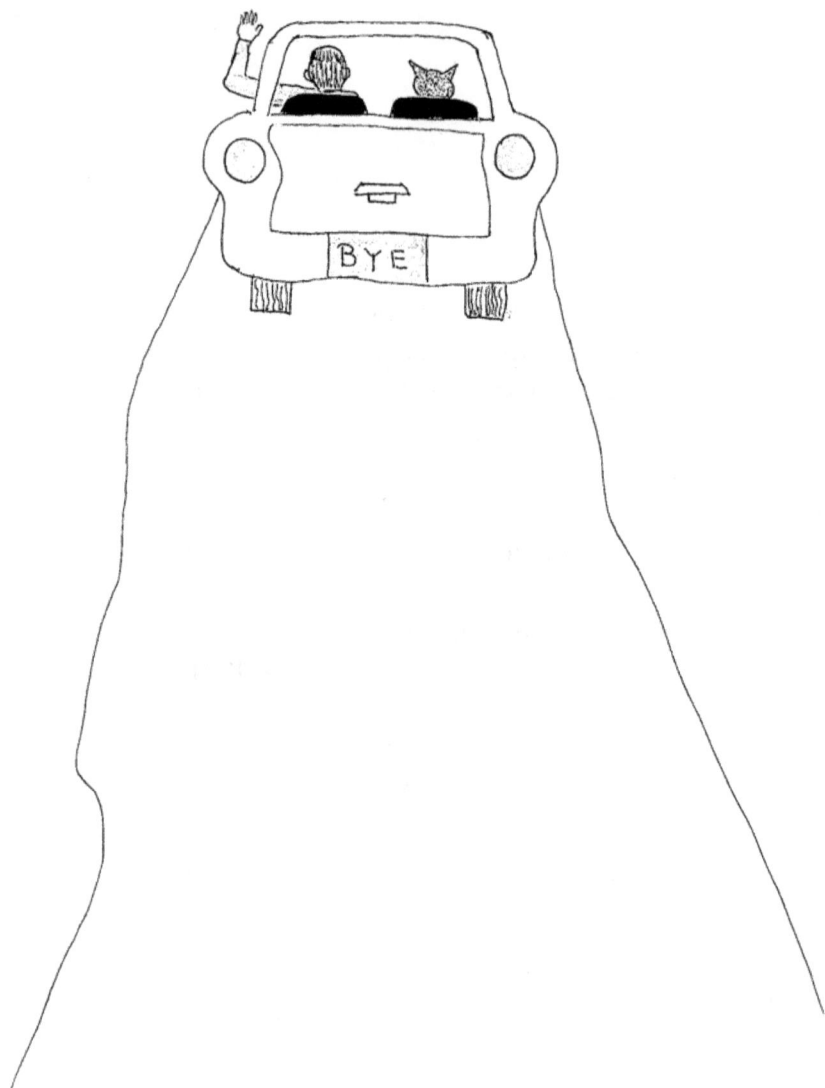

Exiles

Exiles

I imagine her alone
without me to say to her
I knew what she was thinking
and understood in every way,
as we are each exiles from
that place we loved,
banished from what we
thought was a home.

Is there such a place for the unwanted?

We've each been exiled before.
It's a feeling everybody knows
even for the slightest term,
like those pilgrims from England
expunged from what was home.
Wear your exile well, my friend,
and discover new continents
for you and I are like two
lonely stars in the black sky.
Everything is moving, touching,
careening through time,
waiting for a place in the sun—

It's such a fleeting perception . . .

—2002

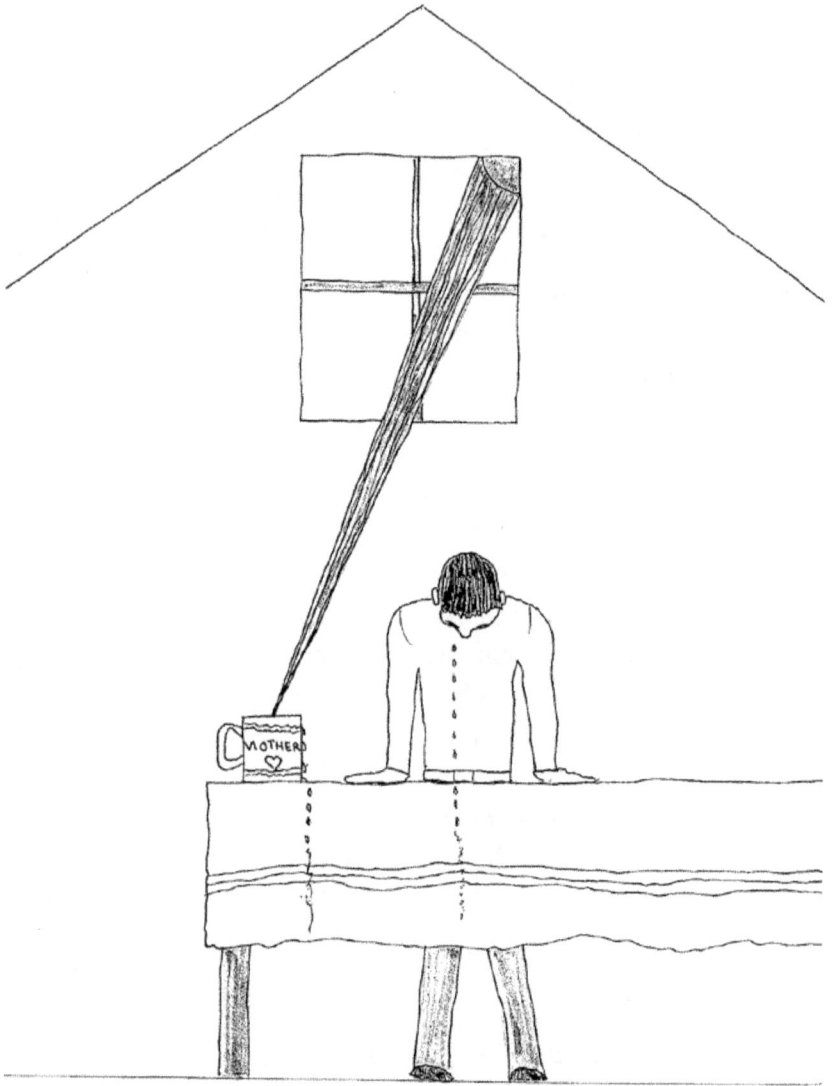

Droplet

Droplet

A drop slides slow and silent
down the slippery glass
never to fire the spirit,
only to see it pass.
It flows beyond the flower,
over the olive stem,
wets the fine white linen
down beyond the hem,
a journey of those bridges
that trace until they dry
joined by each clear droplet
from this shaded eye.

—1990

Dog Days

Dog Days

A stuffy haze
pressed our fate—
summer's phase
for one to hate.

Smells will rise
with a musky tang
that we'll despise
'til thunder's bang.

Even a frog's
lily denies
the days of dogs
in cloudy skies.

With this impurity,
life has a sound,
a noble maturity
growing profound.

—1988

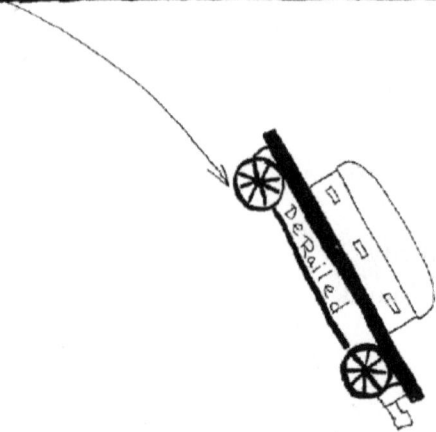

Derailed

Derailed

A morning train passed
like some giant snake
winding through our town
the front end hissing
and back end rattling,
the cars in between
carrying the things
to define our life and
built to haul large loads
over shiny tracks.
Maybe small to start—
engine to each car,
adding as it moves
to build from afar.
Not so different
from our very track
traveled each day
wherever it started
to distant stations.

Why not see until
that known image
along the way has
appeared to vanish?
We pause and wonder,
"Where has that spark gone?"
It seemed much older
then—the paper read,
Derailed from Orange . . .

They melt down the engine,
the red rusted steel to
a steamless heart pale blue
to make some bright new way—
a much better version
to pass the time faster,
not to remember hope
or to give thoughtful pause
for the nostalgia there
beyond the bend of causes.

—2010

Family Album

Family Album

Then
much younger
faces and ink
blot mustaches
drooped around lips
like mirrored commas
around a question
all but asking.

Now
I know
my ken's insufficient—
humanity, worldliness is
nothing but basic survival—
short, dramatic, defensive
photographic sentences,
black on glossy paper,
momentary
visages.

Tomorrow,
non-captioned words
possibly ooze from mustaches
showing frozen reminders of
how little I ever knew
then and now.

—1988

Four Hours

Four Hours

"When kittens are born," she told me,
"the mother teaches them everything —
how to clean our fur, how to eat,
how to hunt various prey, and how to play.
We learn how to share and how to fight.
Sometimes you win. Sometimes you lose.
Mostly, you learn what you are, and
you trust nothing in this world."
"With us it is much different," I said.
"The learning takes many years.
We are babies for several years,
so we learn the basics as you do,
then pre-school, twelve years of formal education,
college, military, post-grad schools, —
there are many different routes.
Then we work at our trade.
It is an extremely long process."
She looked dumbfounded. "I'll say!
So when did you know?"
"Know what," I asked.
"When do you know what you are!"
"Sometimes not for twenty-five to thirty years,
and sometimes we never know!"
"I'm glad I'm a cat," she answered.
"I knew when I was four."
"Four years old," I smiled.
"NO!" she spit.
"Four days?" I questioned.
"Four hours!" she answered.
"You knew four hours after birth!"
"Yes."
"You have to tell me more than yes."
"I knew at that very moment of my
life that I was a cat."
"That's it. You knew you were a cat."

How about you?

"Yes. It's something you don't know."
"I know you're a cat."
"But you don't know about being one."
"About being a cat?"
"Yes."
"What about it?"
"Well, you just know certain things."
"Like what?"

"First, the basics of the life cycle;
  next, my—our place in the natural world."
"Four hours for that!"
"Yes. How about you?"
"Us, well, I'm not sure when we know."
"I know," she said, "so let's look at you,
for example. No preschool for you, then
twelve years of formal education
which you got though—barely. Then
four years of military training and duty,
again by the skin of your teeth, then
college for four years. You did well.
Then a year of postgraduate education,
which you tagged with the word 'bogus,'
then forty years in the working world.
That's about right, isn't it?"
"Yes."
"And you and your species still don't know."
"What? We know everything!"
"Everything except what?"
"What do you mean?"
"Except what I learned in four hours."
                                    —2014

Four in the Afternoon

Four in the Afternoon

There'll be other days in time
when I can write and form my rhyme.

Today just isn't in its place.
It appears I have a rat to race.

Patience better find me soon.
It's already four in the afternoon,

and I'm feeling mad with nothing to say
about this miserable rotten day.

—1989

FOG

oblivion

Fog

Fog

Found a habit, made it my wife.
For me, it was a liquid life.
I drank until I began to spill
like a plant upon a windowsill.

More and more I would envision
bars that held me in that prison.
How could I find the thought
so thirsty after every drought?

One could laugh at such an enigma.
One could cry, knowing the stigma —
all the reasons I would drink,
the most important to happily sink.

To avoid responsibility
the bottom is a place to be,
chasing slop for such a hog,
losing life in freedom's fog.

It isn't wrong to say imbibe.
Many do and stay alive
If like me, your soul must sip
that fog will never lose its grip.

—1987

Green Glass

Green Glass

for my mother

We searched for green glass,
frost-worn clover from
the palm of Nature's hand
as empty shells echoed
within a hall of perfect sound,
a pitch as long as seaweed waves
on sand.

Juxtaposing monuments,
sand fleas bubbled home
at each footstep as
pipers traced prophecies in
palm prints across the strand,

and in that time we walked
away . . .

I understood
new waves cleanse the shore,
and I found some man's refuse —
a discarded piece of green glass,
a dull edgeless gem,
a multitude of greens,
man's envy mocking Nature,
man's greed forming solid
sand to broken glass
to a honed shape as
a gem that fills our jar,
each piece a shrine to
another time,
a legacy as if
heritage were tangible.

Now
the sailor is quenched,
the sea satisfied while
I keep these tombstones to remember
my mother as she stood beyond the
rocks
looking for green glass.

—1992

83

Refuse

Refuse

We send away what we don't want
that holds the things, that must contain—
which may appear as if they aren't
easily viewed to be mundane.

A coconut shell, it may seem,
contains the milk and meat to eat
as it grows in a life-form dream,
like words grow poetry in feet.

And other shapes on roadsides born
may mimic the banana's peel,
like objects they create in form
to lie beyond the simple wheel.

We send away what we have used.
Each vessel ships our grubbing greed,
but as this gold will stay to bruise
ancestral heirlooms of each deed.

In time, it's not as you might think,
what stands for all that we are worth
to count your pennies to the brink
but refuse in the heart of Earth.

—2021

Impossible

Impossible

The sun rises one more time
as always it is *to be*
light unveiling another fall
as well as spilling destiny.
Night tries to seal the past
and sleep is just a way —
a hiatus meant to illustrate
the monuments we stay.
Sometimes managing distance,
but hardly bridging despair,
to me, it's why some mornings
darkness lingers there.
Unable to catch the promises
that gravity defies.
I've been looking for those rainbows
and chasing butterflies,

I know I'm on the border
beginning to understand
that what was denied the child
is impossible for the man.

                            —1987

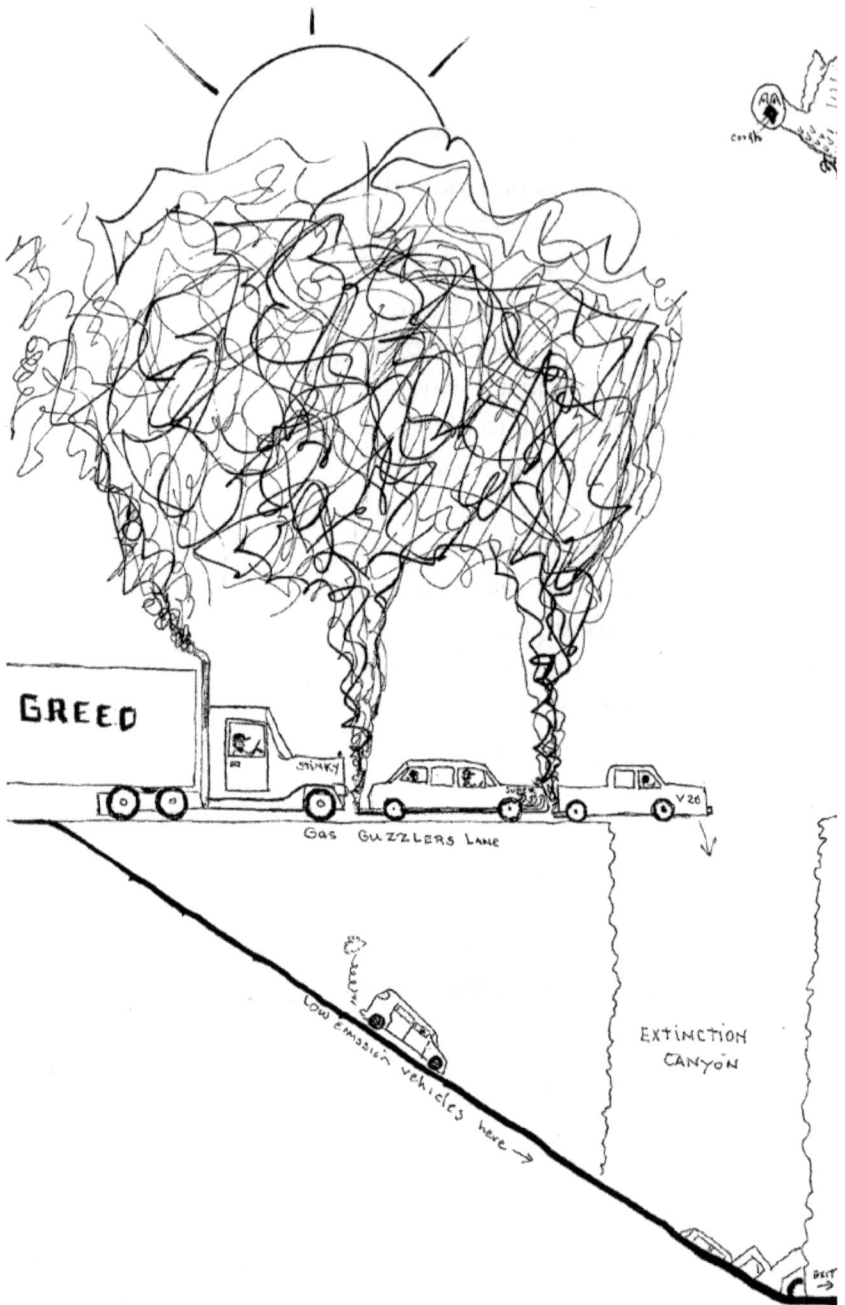

It Must Be a Race

It Must Be a Race

With restrictions loosened,
my wife said, "gazebo weights,"
handed me a coupon, so
I grabbed my mask and
headed over to the next town,
ten miles on a divided highway.

In the slow lane, I realized—
something had changed!

I sped up to my usual
    sixty-three mph
while other vehicles passed me
as if they'd flicked a turnstile
at Grand Central Station on a
Friday evening before a holiday.
The change was in those lunatics,
many traveling eighty in a
    fifty-five, bumper-
to-bumper worse than
    I remembered.

My little car swayed in
    turbo winds
as even eighteen-wheelers
    barreled by me,
none of them gave a glance.

"It must be a race," I said aloud.
"It's a race!"
Of course—space race,
    weapons race,
but we never go fast toward peace
or speed up to save the planet.
Perhaps now it was a human race.
It's going somewhere very fast,
and the fastest ones would win.
They'd be where they wanted to
be
an hour before they needed
    to be late.
Suddenly, I wasn't
    in a hurry.

I slowed my little Fit to
    fifty-seven mph.
I didn't like or want that race,
just gazebo weights and home.

Later, I overheard a conversation.
Someone said the race was for
    extinction . . .
                                    —2020

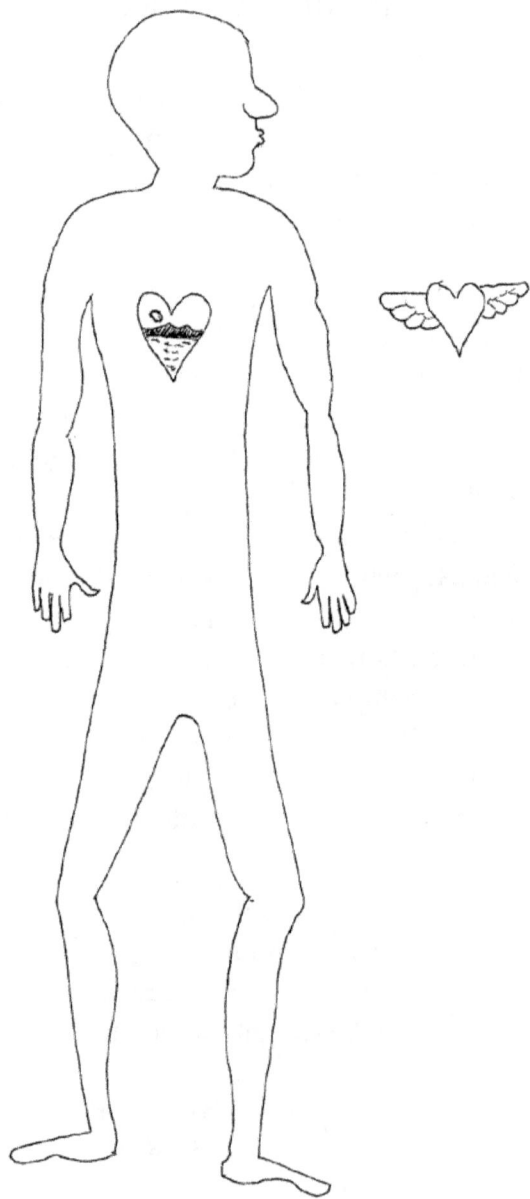

Key

Key

Everyone has a key
within themselves
unlocking monuments,
clocking timelessness,
wading through aqua
on bleached bones,
coral shoulders,
heavy breezes —
holding down
soft sapid evenings
beneath starless heavens,
sun-polished indigo
where the moon
answers

—1994

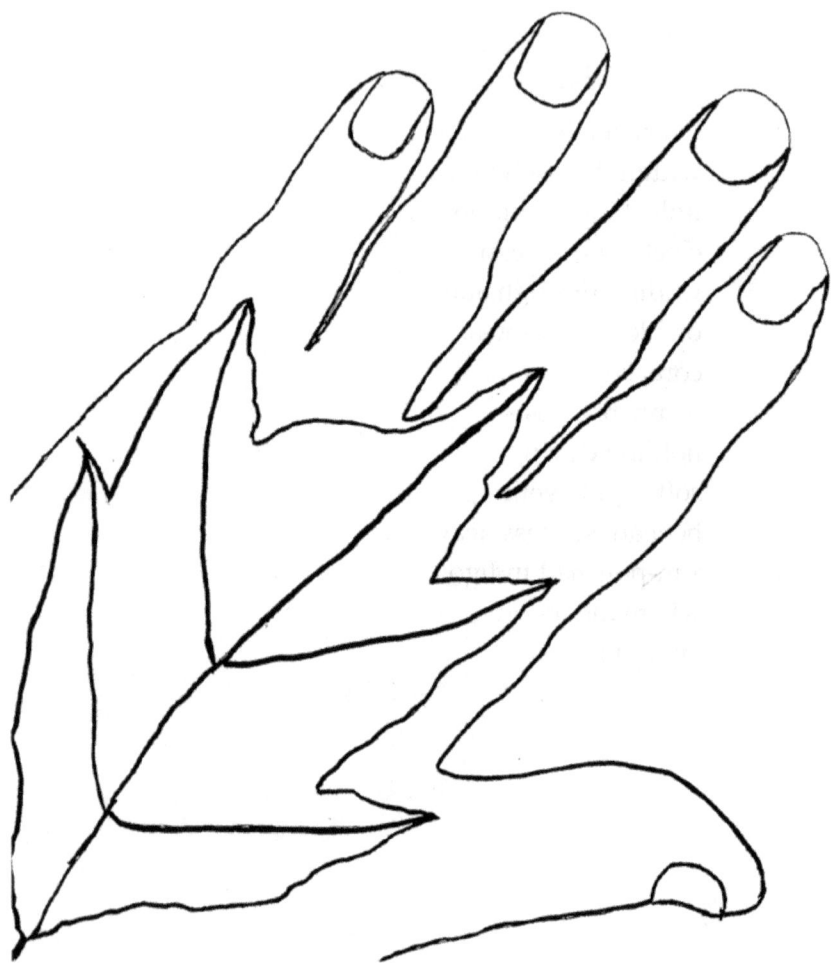

Leaf

Leaf

Veined fingers grasping for
the flatness of earth,
losing as the tumbleweed does
and curled with the ages,
a fist against the wind
like paper skipping on concrete
only to knock on the door
of oblivion.

—1974

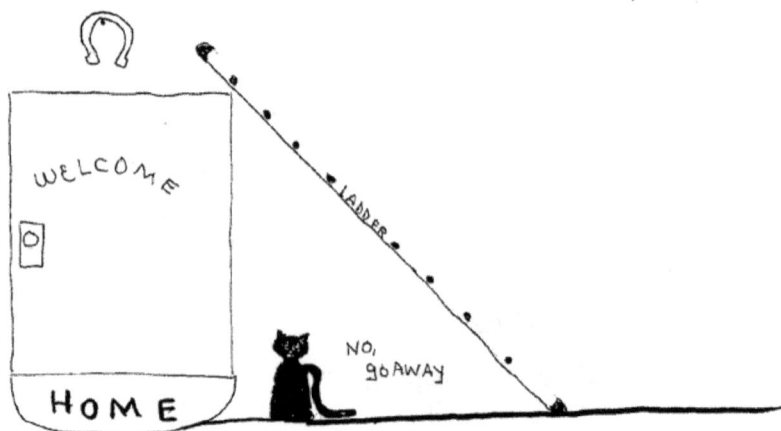

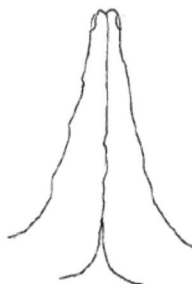

Luck

Some say luck
has a skill:
wear this or that
to bend its will.

Or those who hope
and always swear
upon the leg from
some old hare

or them arranging
a door and shoe,
one over the other—
a nail will do

or how some pray.
"God, can't you see?
Send me luck.
I'm on one knee,"

or how best avoid
an under ladder,
a black cat's lane,
or a mirror's shatter.

Others say, well,
it comes and goes.
What I think is—
no one knows!

But for you dolts
not believing its call,
I hope you have
no luck at all!!!

—1988

It is . . .

It is . . .

Sometime in the night, awakened by the strain of
    meandering fluid,
I sat for lack of sight and light. I felt her soft whiskers
    tickle my ankles.
I ran my hand down to touch her. It made me shiver,
as if the night moved and some unforeseeable switch
    turned to a soft ruffling sound.

The hum was to my left, closer to the bed.
I saw her at the top of the stairs, where a
night-light silhouette showed her like every cat ancestor
    since tar pits.
"Come with me," she said. "Let's play!"
She leaped down the stairs. "Follow me!"
I actually thought about following her, she made it sound
    so good.
Her pointed ears appeared once more.
"Come on!" she said *"Come on!"*
My eyes closing, I looked at my bed. The ebony was
    enveloping me.
"Come onnn!" I heard her feet gallop down the hall, but
    sleep was
the night in me.

I felt those supple paws upon my chest. "Are you coming?"
    she asked, kid-like.
I felt the bed give way and heard her land like a leaf lands
    atop blades of
grass— almost whispering—"the night is . . . " She started
    again.
Down the stairs, she called back to me, "SO BEAU-TI-FUL!"
My eyelids were warmly sealed.
"Yes," I answered, "It is . . . "

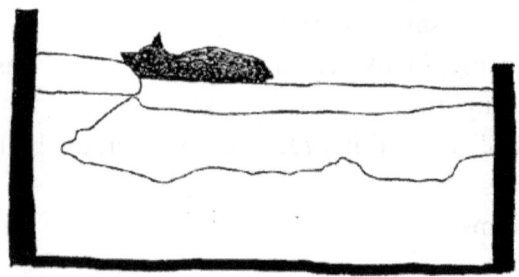

"It is . . . "

I opened my eyes to find her curled against me.
Daylight powdered its chalk eraser onto night.
The room appeared as some blackboard equation, all angles,
    a marriage of black and white.
Before I left for work, I pulled the blankets about her
    shoulders — she was
    idling and blinking at me.
From the top of the stairs, I turned and said,
"Come on. The Day is so Wonderful!"
She blinked at me, blinked that my question seemed quite
    passionless, and
blinked again, closing her eyes.
"But, yes," she answered, "It is . . . "

— 1997

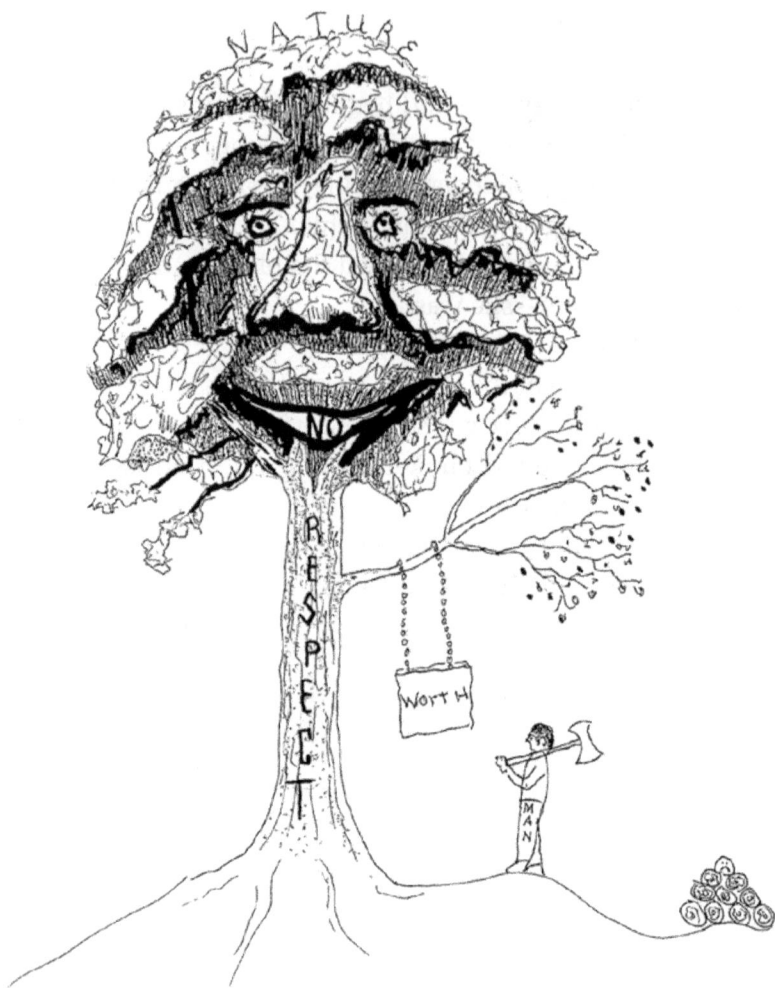

Worth

Worth

Me, I like to non-conform,
and criticize those politics,
maybe even cause a storm
to see the monkeys do their tricks.

Every master has command
of the bitterness in my soul,
crushing wills with evil hands
to force us to a different role.

I fight the battle every day,
face a path that's overgrown.
It's confusing what these idiots say,
depraved to what is really known.

Waking, one must thank the Earth
and honor Nature as our bearer.
How does one earn such worth
by what is seen in the mirror?

—1978

" I SAW
The best minds
of my Generation
destroyed by
Madness "

Howl

Howl

I can smell those sweet books
from my car on the street.
Sound pages flit in my ear,
ranking me incomplete.

The door shuts behind me —
a bookstore restaurant,
my mind cycles inward,
the sight of shopping carts
filled with groceries –
I think,
"Supermarket in California."
All time hails to Ginsberg
in the poesy section
a day after his death.
So cosmopolitan
for such a country lad,
a boy as daft as me,
at something so complex.
to muse death in earnest.

A wall of books spilled
vibrant circus colors.
I'm not a beat guy, but
those lines surface as
Seuss-like horns blared,
suddenly deafening
as I begin to rive
"Howl" from memory.

                                    — 1997

Better

Better

The week was finally over,
and I had had enough.
It was busier than usual.
We were buried in work stuff.

With spring now arriving,
I anticipated more.
My thoughts had turned to tennis,
and I was out the door.

Months of working the daylight
from almost dawn to dusk —
now to vent my frustrations.
Oh, yes, I know I must.

Strapping on my Nikes
and donning my favorite shorts,
I took up my mighty scepter
and headed for the courts.

Steve was patiently waiting
turning on his tennis brain.
As I squealed around the corner,
a dozen people craned.

I grabbed my bag of racquets
and stepped in ready to go
just in time to witness
newly falling snow.

Maybe all men shouldn't —
some do and don't know why —
struggle with their emotions
when its better just to cry.

—1991

105

For Our Thirst

For Our Thirst

There are values
that some don't see,
and one of them
is honesty.
Stumble on it
bit by bit,
found to be
afraid of it,
afraid to show
or give with ease
or uncover errs
instead to cease.
To grasp and shake
and perhaps confer,
undoubtedly,
it may not occur.
And in those moments
that come after,
we see it join
with our laughter,
only to realize
it was there at first,
but we drank elsewhere
for our thirst

—1991

Classified

CLASSIFIED
HELP WANTED
IMMEDIATE OPENINGS

We want you!
It says . . .
But do they?
Do they want thoughts?
The child we were?
They want Microsoft . . .
Apple . . .
They want "yes" people
idealess minds
unfamily, benefitless occupants!
Call Now!
Temps to Perm, or direct hire!
Your choice!
We between the lines have
fallen to lawless labors,
lifeless acts where
background is helpful,
experience necessary,
and opinions prohibited.

—1999

Berth

Berth

Harbor light
Ocean night
Waves that bend
To the right

Airy musk
Born of dusk
Salty foam
Sailor's husk

Sand of dune
Time in June
Reflections of
A seashell moon

Boats in line
Make a sign
Pointing to
Berthing time
—1976

PaPa, help!

PaPa, *Help!*

"PaPa, *help!*" she says to me,
this little life I've witnessed
growing my world several sizes.
"PaPa, *help!*" she says again
with her hands raised to me,
so I melt down to her.
She has my heart when
she calls me PaPa—
she knows I'm Grandpa,
but PaPa is her word for me.
And when she says "Help!"
I doubt if I'd feel a concrete wall
as it crumbled from between us,
or when from nowhere
she says, "Kiss," and kisses me
then, "Hug," and hugs me,
I could cry!
All my adversaries might laugh
at a six-time scoring champ,
goon hockey player showing such
weakness and emotion as his
granddaughter says, "Gammy sit,"
patting the floor beside her.
As my wife sits and they color or
fit puzzle piece states in the USA,
I find it better than a perfect sunset.
At "PaPa, *help,*" I'd miss my chance
at heaven's gate!

—2006

Ova / Ideas

Ova/Ideas

In the beginning,
It's growing inside,
a fragile egg
waits to abide.

Shell so thick,
structurally dense,
proud of birthing
something immense.

Rejoice in safety
away from blame,
the shell is trust—
Ova its name.

In time, a crack,
of need to adore,
fate and hope,
foot in the door.

Inside the albumen,
a cognitional fast,
beginning to end,
all things must pass!

It then breaks open,
a thought born late—
nothing is missing
to infuse debate.

Recall sees beyond
wishes or regrets.
Now there's no point
in covering one's bets.

So come here or go on
leaving that shell—
an unanswered question
hatched upon well.

—2011

Fishing

Fishing

We went fishing to catch fish
and to talk man talk as we do.
"Fish!" I said to him.
"Grandson, will they choose
not to bite today?"
After a moment, he replied,
"That's what you say about
my generation. We choose
not to!"

"True," I answered as air filled
my lungs as if a bellows blew into me,
fanning flames to a crackling rage.
Inside me red tongues spoke
my father's words. Oh, and all the
words I wanted to say back to my father,
but couldn't . . .

How the bonfire smoldered when hit
by a bucketful of realization, the fire
thinned like the leaves in the stream bed,
as if water could wear away my scorn
for temperance . . .

"Yes," I said. "It's what we
all want you to have,
choices . . . "

He gave me the strangest look.
I guess he taught
me something after all.

—2020

In Migration

In Migration

echoing "Ovenbird" by Robert Frost
"The Darkling Thrush" by Thomas Hardy

Evening walk, homage to our sun
like fire, it graces autumn's hue
to be decorated by a hardy frost.
Crisp decay smolders, and
dusk obscures the path
so that I have to kneel
to find my way
when I hear a word
in "Crescendo!"

"Teach," it says. "No."
"Teach'er" echoes from anonymity,
then darts beyond the rippling auburn sea.
I see it!
Sculling across a crescent of sun,
seeming to chase the horizon
then fold its wings to oblivion
beneath pastel into umber.
In its fall, I wished I'd asked,
"What darkness is a bird
in migration?"

—1994

Of Hearts . . .

Of Hearts . . .

for Diana

England is my second country,
my second life,
my twin soul.
I remember being English.
Today the price was dear!

I watched the shadow of a rose
beneath a spirit's wing
cast itself upon her roads
and across all the roads of the world,
the length and breadth of benevolence.

I feel the burden of guilt,
of wanting to watch in death
the life I watched in hope — to
behold the God-made being doomed
and the manmade be consumed.

Perhaps we witnessed
the essence
of a
dream

and how

naivety dies like a future Queen.
                              —1997

Ode to the Company

Ode to the Company

Life in dust,
lost in turn—
only rust
to live and learn.
No open doors
or stairway climb—
only floors
of ancient rhyme.
There we dwell
on promised hope—
no one to tell,
no way to cope.
Successes found
will never be
in a place that's bound
for obscurity.

—1981

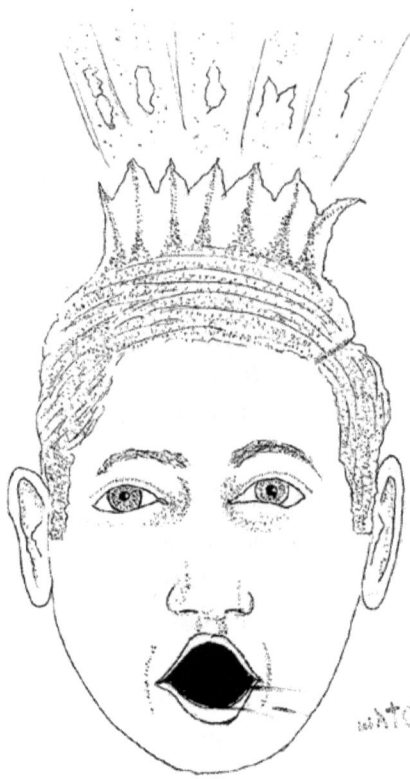

Ode to a Crabby Soul

Ode to a Crabby Soul

Watch out for me—I'm crabby!
I'll bite your head off today!
I'd probably knock down little kids
if they got in my way!

Everything makes me angry,
and what doesn't has me cross.
I'm impatient with my manner
so don't bug me—just get lost!

If you want to ask a question,
make sure that it has weight.
If you bug me with some nonsense,
I'll pound you through that gate.

I'm really wishing for something
that will crazily make me pop.
In a mood like this, the only good thing
is finally blowing my top!

—1991

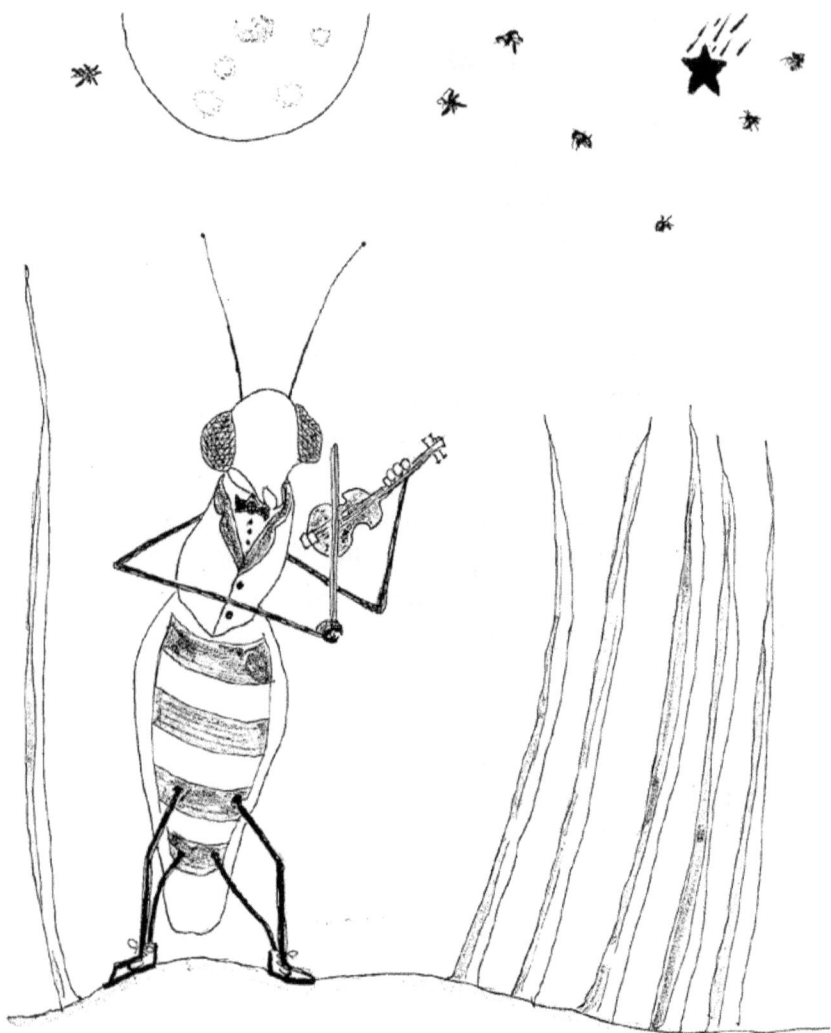

Night to Pass

Night to Pass

This is my oldest poem.
All others are lost forever.

Crickets chirp on a
drizzling night.
They seem to cheer
the absence of light.
They'll settle down
nestling grass,
sounding the seconds for
the night to pass.

—1971

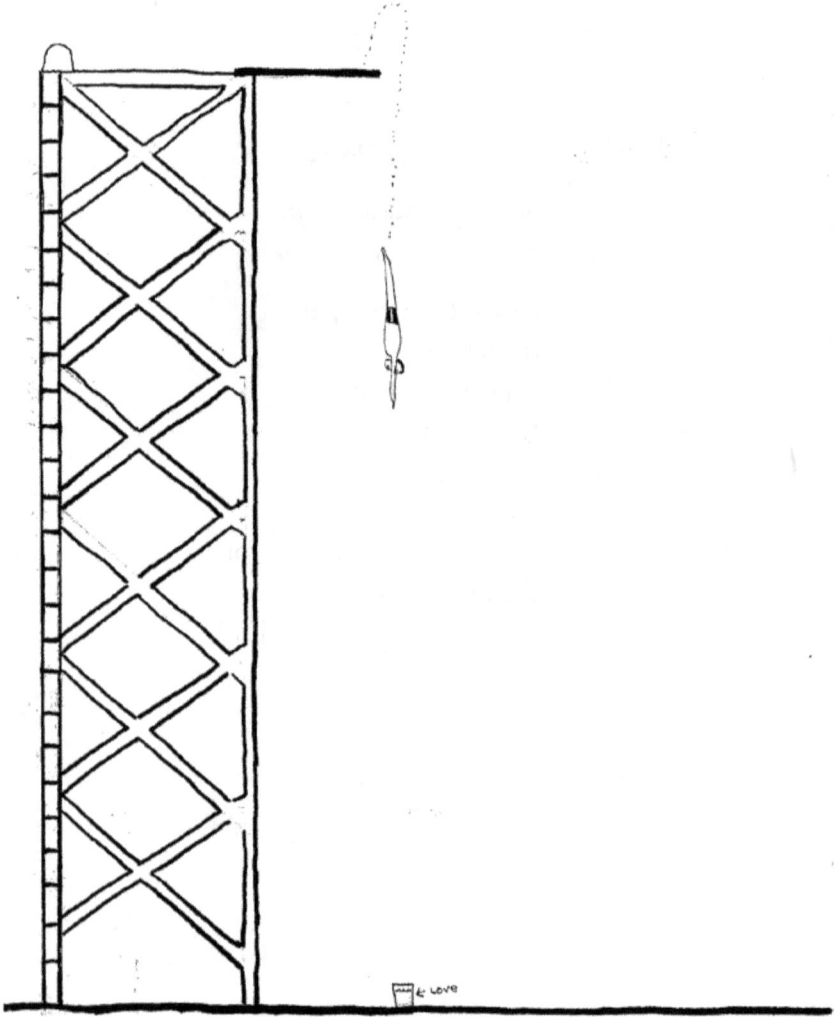

Never Been This Far Before

Never Been This Far Before

Should I fear what's in store?
I've never been this far before.
Once, all that was me stayed inside,
but a soulful force now tugs my tide.

All those secrets speaking-wise
with solemn, staring, glinted eyes,
what I should do I see some more.
I've never been this far before.

For in your eyes could be as far
as I could be and know we are.
From there, I see beyond this place
past your brow and pretty face.

There lies Eros in separate lines,
yet he multiplies and intertwines.
Now love's facet joins me to trace
you arched in form to my embrace.

I proclaim to legions of love's living lore.
I'm so much farther than I've been before.

—1986

Nature

Nature

How does her resilience stand
upon our constant show and show?
Is Nature's foe an annexed man
who strikes upon her blow by blow?

Does she fall each year in prelude?
Do we burn and scorch her eyes?
Why do we know each way to kill
but always question why we die?

Evidence answers that query once
with the beauty of an ashen earth.
There the inquisition stands
juxtaposing dust and birth.

Ice may freeze and heaven scorn
in subtle hues and deep blues.
Perhaps in rebirth flesh will know
those which are the basic rules.

Man's deed for Earth is narrow proof
as Nature claims the rent in truth.

—2004

Money World

Money World

A tractor on a farm furrows
earth's brown water
into rich waves

unlike the nearby neighbor
on a broken swing in
sunless shadows on
the crisis of hope —

desiring needs
in order to build
fate from an
emptiness.

Beyond that . . .
only the lasting memory
of flourishing fields and
distant hills.
All that countered by
a depository vault and
piles of bills stacked high
row after row.
Money divides by
unjust means.
Birthrights make gods
of buyers and sellers
of haste and waste.

Desires separate
value from time
borrowed
as if
Nature
had a choice!
                    — 2010

T. Christopher F. O'Brien
USMC Lance Corporal
1st Marine Div, 3rd Bat.
October 30, 1945 - July 9, 1967
Died of wounds from hostile
Small arms Fire - Quang Nam
Provence, South Vietnam

Purple Heart
Combat action Ribbon
National Defense Service Medal
Vietnam Campaign Medal
Vietnam Service Medal
Marine Corp Presidential Unit Citation
Vietnam Gallantry Cross
Marine Good Conduct Medal
Marine Corp Expeditionary Medal

"My Brothers"

"My Brothers"

"My brothers," I said aloud,
my fingers on line 23E of panel 39:
T. Christopher O'Brien
halfway up.

Staring back at me, a hunched
hallowed, silver-haired soul
looking as if he belonged there
and leaning to help
hold that ground
but feeling guilty,
guilty, but lucky,
very lucky, indeed.

Chris was a hero. He lived
United States American:
athlete, scholar, patriot, friend
now forever young.
I remember you!
Later, we saw the guard changing.
Their faces became his face
the unknown suddenly known.
That futile edge of earth,
that furrowed wall wasn't
holding back any longer.
The names, an intricate structure,
each a brace threaded as one to
reflect upon those waters
a place to move forward
and never to forget—
we remember you . . .

—2002

135

FUTURE

Purge

Purge

Another wave
Approaches the coast
Spilling forth
Its foamy boast
So far to look
No further to see
The first one breaks
Far beyond me
I'm there to shoulder
All this emotion
Testing the currents
In the midst of an ocean
Catching the sun
Drinking the rain
Dispersing my dreams
A cleansing refrain
Now I weigh
A distance far greater
Something between us
Sooner not later
So I may end
As each wave before
Destined to purge
All over some shore

—1986

Doom

Doom

In moody times like these,
when I brood instead of think,
makes me want to find
that one and only drink:

climbing down the day
beyond the afternoon
like a solemn sinking sun
relinquished to its doom.

—1987

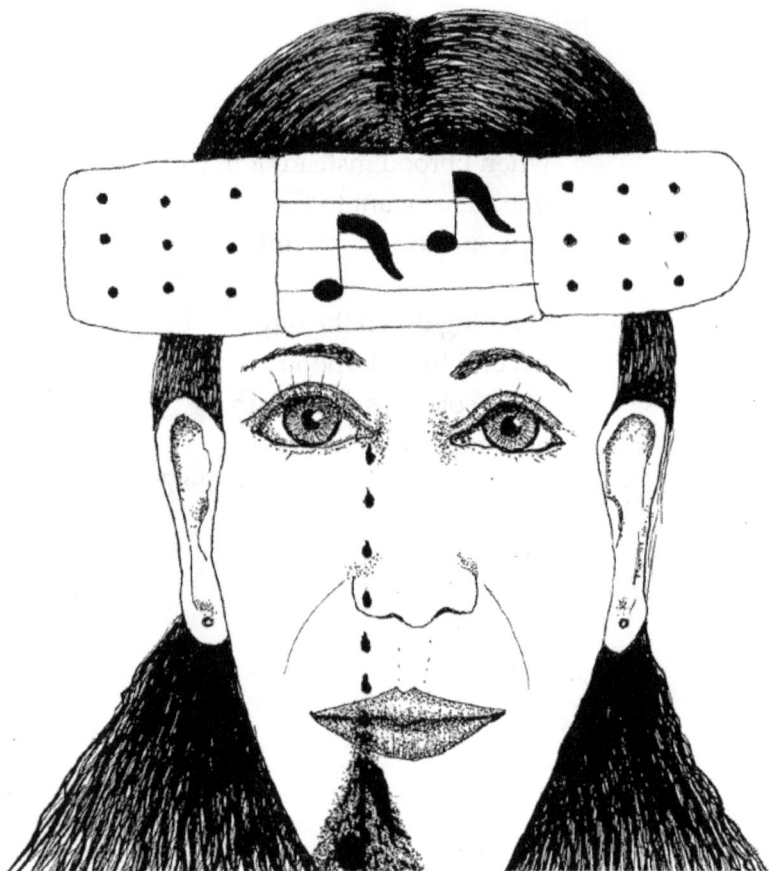

A Song Can Heal Itself

A Song Can Heal Itself

Not if this song would play
once I received your text—
only if in long days
when you'll visit us next.

I hear notes in a voice
upon my thoughtful ear
and know you're right to say,
"True beauty's always near."

The song—a mind in tune—
found kindness in my sleep.
All day long, I'm singing
words memories can keep.

A tune never to wane,
joy reprises so long.
It will always compound
our twin souls ever strong.

How music stays within
quiet times on our shelf.
It tells what no one knows—
a song can heal itself.

—2021

Sibyl

Sibyl

I have studied Michelangelo's
painting of Sibyls on a ceiling,
prophetesses in knowing,
queens in the realm of dream.
I knew such a soul.

Once, deep within the wood at my
country home, the green-eyed seer
existed,
soothsaying seasonal sounds into
unspoken oracles of honest
understanding and immeasurable
loyalty from her place at my desk.

Whether I had written well
or not, she remained. I provided
her space — so, she'd leave the
mice by my slippers.

$$-1994$$

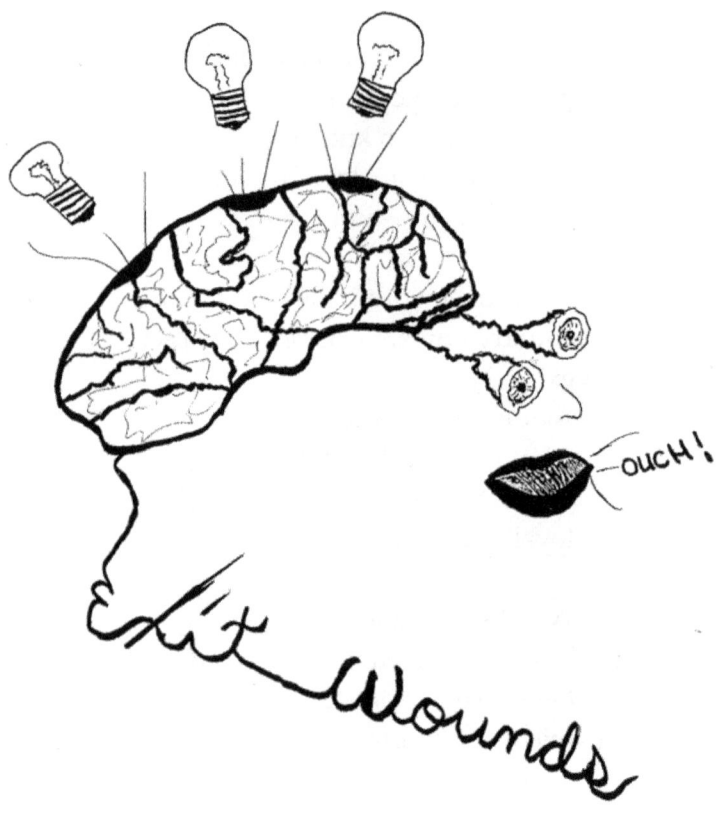

Exit Wounds

Exit Wounds

Sometimes, ideas are like wounds.
They leave a mark on you,
a place you are conscious of
as you overlook other concerns.
Then a transformation occurs.
The wound scabs over,
subtly reminding you it's still there.
How it kinetically cues knowledge
so your awareness changes.
It grows less familiar day by day.
You'd see it as a blemish, then
you might remember what it was.
Yet, the tiny cells made repairs,
got themselves right again
but somehow couldn't match colors
precisely enough until some months
or perhaps years later.

Ideas, like scars, change us,
and if you don't honor them,
you'll never know . . .

$-$2004

Fit to Live

Fit to Live

*Part of the American Dream is to live long
and die young. Only those Americans who are
willing to die for their county are fit to live.*
— General Douglas MacArthur

I've never been able to explain
my emotions when she was born,
how it brought you home to us
if only for some moments torn.

Her time was special being born.
It taught us warriors how to cope.
I clung to her within my arms
and sought her eyes for lasting hope.

I saw her pupils as colored flags,
parade ground reminiscence caught.
Never dip Old Glory too low —
for peace we fight, the battle fought.

For me, that time you were away
this soldier swore an oath and more.
Fight for your country, "be fit to live!"
and pray the soldiers back from war.

I love freedom in a baby's eyes.
I respect the hues that she will see.
I hope she sees a peace enjoyed
as do the robins in my cherry tree.

— 2004

Earth's Fall

Earth's Fall

A bird doesn't know about newspapers
just as a hero would not question "but must."
She searches for food and sings with hope
And, unable to trust, follows her heart.

She's hunter and hunted, Nature and guts.
She'd never acknowledge a forest defaced.
Her soul is Nature's name for devotion,
and this is a time for poise and grace.

I heard her song above the barren hills
on Sunday's hike in a Mount Warwick wood.
Along the clear-cut shoulders of the trail,
her song was where her home once stood.

How can we who aid in Earth's fall
enjoy her sacrifice to build some wall?

—2005

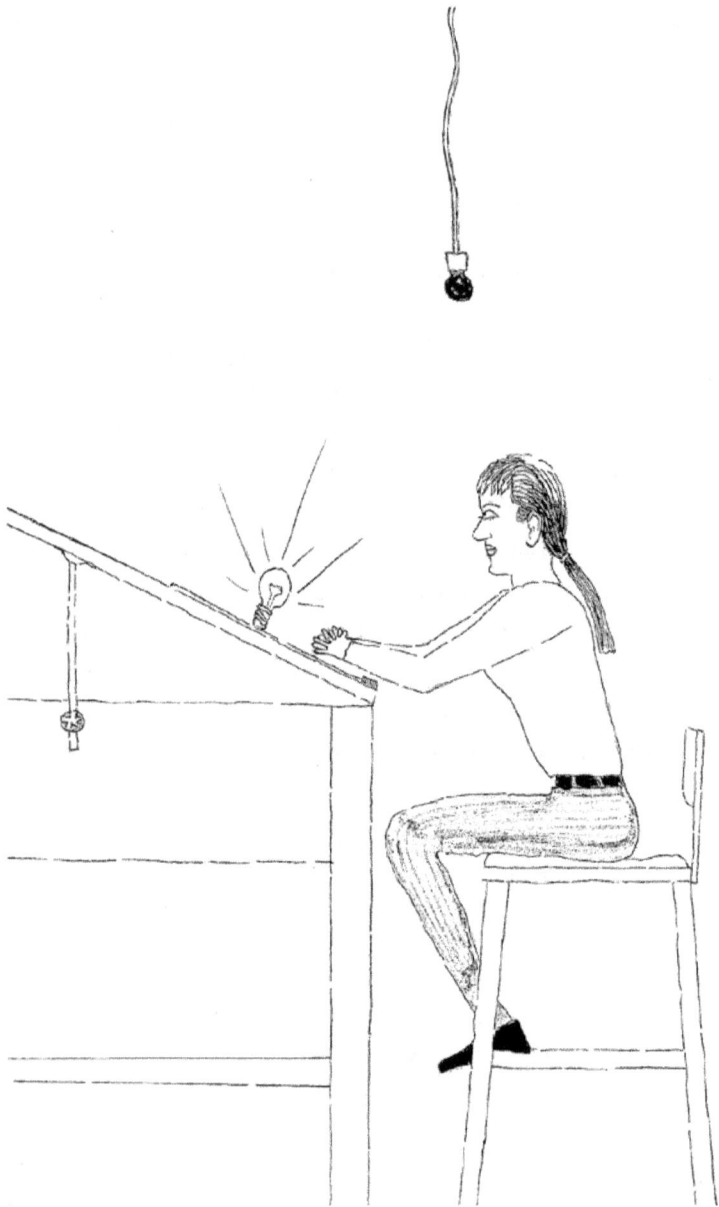

Need

Need

Wanting things one can have
without understanding need?
Need is about every day
but not the same as greed.

It has its bare necessities
laid out in a straight line,
the boss of all desires
no interim hope to find.

Someone will tell of need,
but it's really just, "I want it!"
For need you must truly bleed
and never, ever flaunt it!

I need creation moments.
They turn me inside out
to unearth another purpose,
an idea that's most devout.

To take that something somewhere
and hope it turns to art
on the trail of lost causes—
new notions beat my heart.

Not what I have written
or how to manage rhyme,
but what one finds in between
each and every line . . .

—2020

Secret Countenance

Secret Countenance

A woman needs in terms!
Independent thinking too!
If you believe in this idea,
if you understand about fate
or how she paid you attention
or how she gave and you took,
you have a chance in love, man!
For she will always give you more!

It's an unbalanced scale
or a secret countenance
not made in artful disillusions
but of unbroken promise.

A broken heart isn't your calling.
It is not impossible to choose.
Observe beauty not as a face,
for love is not what you think.
It's not about angry tolerance,
It is more than ever imagined!

If the fates are smiling, she
will love your flaws and foibles.

If not, as a gentlemen, it is wise to
fall upon your sword!

—2002

Snake

Snake

inspired by "Snake"
by D. H. Lawrence

A summer's day so warm
with heat alone to take
made me think of Lawrence
and his verses on the snake.
I, too, have waited my turn
to many a serpent's slither.
Each shocking introduction
puts me past a dither!
I've tried to become familiar
with their gentle flowing grace,
as always it's that wriggle
that starts this heart to race.
Not for fear of harm,
I know that I am stronger —
hell, that in just one arm,
perhaps it's even longer.
Then why be so afraid
crossing with this creature?
Should my bros be to blame
or some late creepy feature?

So each time I break the rules
and strike havoc on the snake,
as with Lawrence, there's regret
that I know I must forsake.

—1987

155

Salome

Salome

Inevitably, morning came and,
like a pinball, I bounced downstairs
to be greeted by that cat —
I hate that cat!
She looks at me as though
I am indebted to her.
I really think someday she will talk and
her mouth will form words instead of
her long irritating cries for attention.

The sun caught her silhouette on the chair back
as she directed her regal gaze at me.
"Shut up," I said instead of *"Good morning."*

I walked away only to be greeted by her in the kitchen.
Weaving through a maze of chair and table legs,
she appeared at my feet with monotonous meows.
The only escape was to scratch her belly —
she would have her way or none at all.
I, being of stubborn nature, would never give in —
not me, I hate cats or even touching them.
I stepped over her many times on my way
to the refrigerator and a glass of juice.

All the time, I kept telling myself,
pat her and you will be free of this
purring ball and chain.
I drank my juice and reached down
almost to her head but paused.
"Drop Dead," I said and
walked out of the house on
unfavorable terms with the
Queen of Siam.

$$-1972$$

Sailors of Darkness

Sailors of Darkness

for the lost sailors

An alley with its angles,
brick walls upon cement—
there the bodies tangle
where garbage will be sent.

I, too, could have tumbled
like paper in the wind
rolling in the shadows
against the dirty walls of sin.

That glow may be a comfort,
but it can't replace the sea,
the courage for deep water
or a sailor's destiny.

In darkness and oppression,
pride can't make them stop.
They exchange the very fluids.
They value to the drop.

In amongst the ash cans,
the barrels, and debris
lie those tattered sailors
lost in Liberty

—1988

Rainy Nights

Rainy Nights

How darkness came running,
in a stride quickly sped,
emerging in the light
that lit the stop sign red.

Quickly the form appeared.
More quickly was it gone.
Leaving soft sound patterns,
the runner glided on.

Fog-smoke edged lights
like cars could be surreal
as if the air had moved
and not the blackest wheel.

I gave into my coat,
hunched my hope within,
paused for a moment
I knew would not begin.

I might be there forever
waiting for those lights
that weigh themselves in time
for other rainy nights.

         −1995

Your Robin Is a Hawk

Your Robin Is a Hawk

Found a baby robin.
Thought it was a hawk.
It lay so very helpless,
head upon the block.
Found a cardboard box,
a couple of rags for dust.
Decided to be a hero.
My conscience said I must.
Calling for assistance
to save this red-tailed prince,
the sanctuary answered,
"Bring the hawk at once."
I traveled a great distance.
No farther had I been.
The birdman said, "Hawk?
This babe's a robin!"
Beyond my embarrassment,
I heard, "We take them, too."
I left a place called Quabog
to wonder who was who?
The deed seemed less majestic,
the journey home long on thought.
I wondered if I'd have done it
if I knew that it was not.
In those miles of driving
with such secrets to unlock,
I finally heard a whisper . . .
"Your robin is a hawk!"

—1987

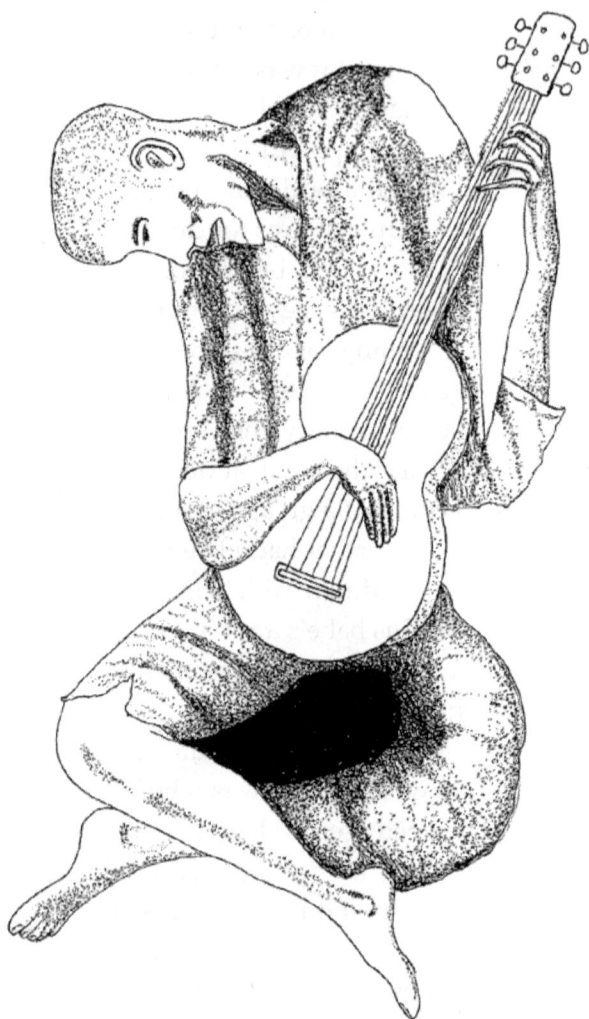

The Da Vinci Code

The Da Vinci Code

When I awoke, Da Vinci was
playing guitar in my living room.
He was a left-handed wizard
with a mop-top Beatle haircut.
"Leonardo, what are you doing here?" —
such an honored guest to play for me!
He just continued to play. He
smiled at me and played an acoustical
version of *Stairway to Heaven*.
In his smile, I somehow grasped
the Mona Lisa smile he'd patted
on canvas five hundred years before —
such a subtle smile, a Madonna
for the tunes he plays me now!

Like all the smiles you gave me true
let me know where I've seen you
must be in the Louvre.

—2005

FEAR

FUTURE

The Edge

The Edge

a balance fine
draws a line
the edge is always in its place
the image never dulls
steps fall sure and short
each a pattern to displace
the edge cuts both ways
in its angle of disgrace
a push
a pull
memory trembles
beyond the edge nothing
as the mystery unfolds
powerless terror found
in a tumble
until ground

from there you see
the edge so clear
and wonder how
it brought such fear

—1990

Queens and Kings

Queens and Kings

A day of reflection, a beautiful eve,
we talked and laughed, nothing to grieve —
a night of family, together we'd fall
down some highway to Ingleside Mall.
We window-shopped and played on moving stairs
up to other floors, up with the lightest cares.
In a window show, four kittens, three black,
drew such a crowd — we were six rows back.
Their image a size, limitless to all
a gargantuan innocence, our hearts do recall . . .
Freedom was gaping from that glass.
How could they exhibit something so vast?

All who watched those queens and kings
found themselves at the end of the string.
We giggled. They danced, knocking each other down
as we left applauding the best show in town.

                                — 1988

Pioneer Valley Drive-In

Pioneer Valley Drive-In

To all the exciting nights
when we watched iconic views
as a summer's pitch-dark eve
posed those golden hues.

Kinetic manmade lightening
would brightly entertain.
Prism-pictured projections
sprayed neon across a plain.

Today, no one would notice
her rusted porous screen,
scars that marked from lifting
what imaginations dreamed.

What captured my nostalgia
might be the nights I'd miss
the giants of the cinema and
thoughts on my first kiss.

Thinking back on those tales,
a coin time's promise tossed.
Computers and cell phones
won't save the world we lost.

So I stand this evening
beyond the construction gate
by a poised Goliath digger
to mourn a loss too late.

                              −1988

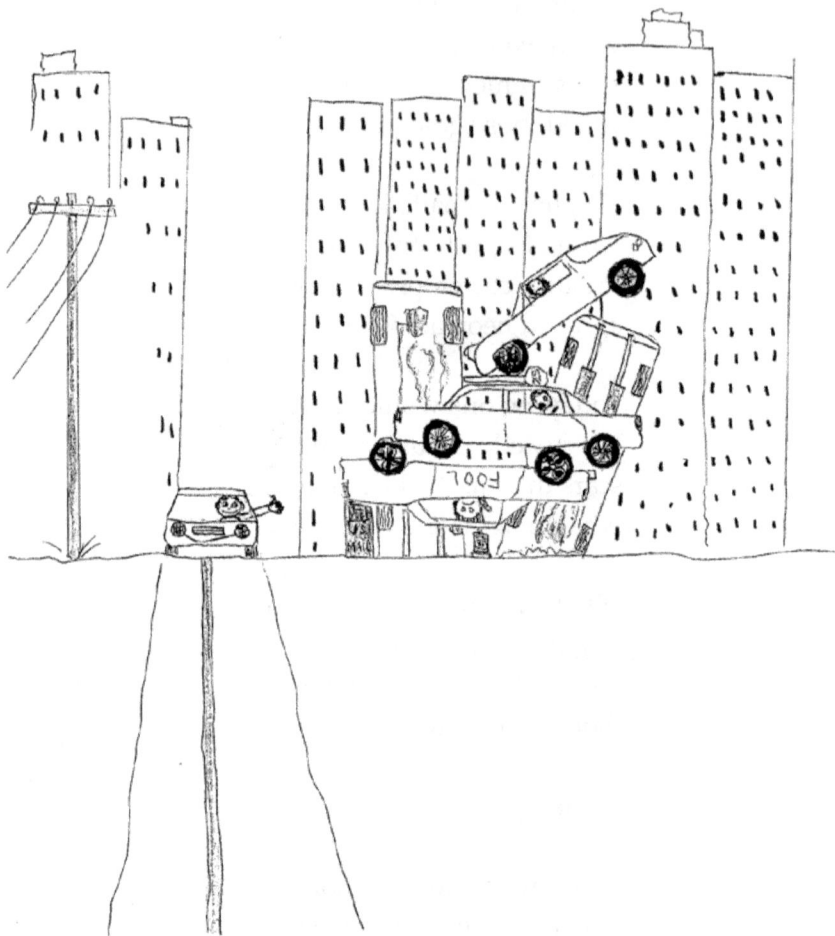

Path of Fools

Path of Fools

On a busy highway today,
I had my mirror in hand
and watched a guy tailgate me.
I waved to him my demand.

His anger went weaving!
At me, he shook his phone —
was yelling and swerving
in speeds of herringbone.

Later,
at the bottom of a ramp
I saw his unlit directive.
Is he turning left or right?
Could his blinker be defective?

How he sped up on yellow,
floored the car on red,
drove through the light
flashing *walk* instead.

Pedestrians dove for safety,
his speed was so intense:
never a cop in sight,
to witness such an offense,

The traffic slowed down
as many sirens encroached,
one lane closed on Main
to the scene I approached.

It was a four-way accident
in the middle of my town.
The same guy was driving,
but his car was upside down.

My moralistic mind thought,
 "In rushing, there is no gain.
"It's possible that he could
plead
"I think I lost my brain!"

Let's say that it is important
to obey all the traffic rules,
and please endeavor to avoid
the dangerous path of fools.

—2019

ROBERT LEE FROST
MAR. 26, 1874 — JAN 29, 1963
"I HAD A LOVER'S QUARREL WITH THE WORLD."

To Be Distinct

To Be Distinct

I went to write it,
but couldn't think
simple enough
to be distinct.
I went to think it
but didn't know
complex enough
to undergo.
The loss of peers
has my sync!
Of lost innocence,
could we guess
about a time
so conscienceless?
Just a pilgrim
without an age —
some romantic on
a neoclassic page,
eternally nostalgic,
forever displaced,
regrettably cynical
about this race.

So,
I tried to write it
but couldn't think
what requires me
to be distinct.

—1994

My Will

My Will

The change winds know
they come alone to chill,
sweeping in cold and low,
dampening a boy's will.

Whatever life is lighting
reveals in our aging bones,
our bygone memories fighting
since time is on the phone.

Daily dabs of reflection
may see beyond a nose
with wrinkles in inspection,
faces lined in feet of crows.

The secret to my own will
is applying forget-me-nots
and always getting my fill
of those long, long thoughts.

If peers are so short-sighted,
let age measure them in years.
They can act old and blighted
as death whispers in their ears.

−1998

The Glory of the Kite

The Glory of the Kite

It's about letting go.
Fliers often know
how releasing line
can always be refined.

Not too much at first
so flying isn't cursed.
Skies often blur,
and sudden dives occur.

Make decisions quick
as winds attempt to trick.
A twitch of wrist refined
brings a grateful climb.

Fliers fear ceiling's coup,
since it's what they tether to,
but never see the crash —
just a string and paper hash.

—2010

The Insufficient Word

The Insufficient Word

In my mind I question,
"Is love sometimes unfair?"
Inwardly perplexing
thoughts make words despair.

I hoped aged perception
graces unknown art,
bringing out the meaning —
a vocabulary for a heart

beyond infatuation,
testing every doubt,
living an expression
I couldn't live without.

Flawed by thoughts of perfect,
perfection takes my gaze
mirrored in your image —
a value value can't appraise.

Again, I test my patience
with the greatest verb
and engage my litigation
with the insufficient word.

                                        —1982

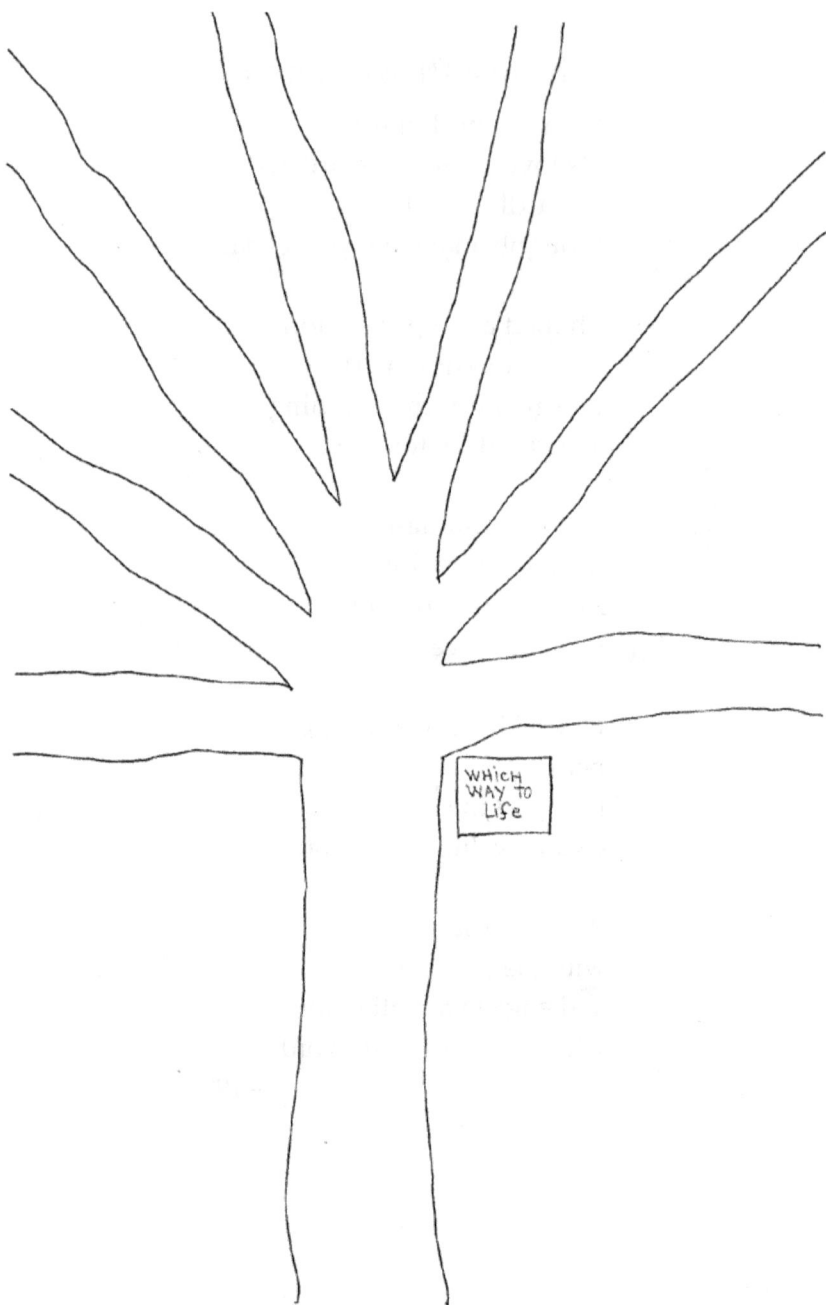

The Crossroads

The Crossroads

Does anyone know the limits
or the exact amount of doubt
for those of us who guess
what others can't figure out?

Does anyone know the feeling
or the form the facts may take
if our disappointment continues?
Those human hearts may break.

Does anyone have justification
for a different road to cruise?
Aren't we at the crossroads
with few other ways to choose?

Does anyone know the answers?
What's beyond the tree-lined bend?
Perhaps it's a new beginning.
We hope it's not the end.

—1984

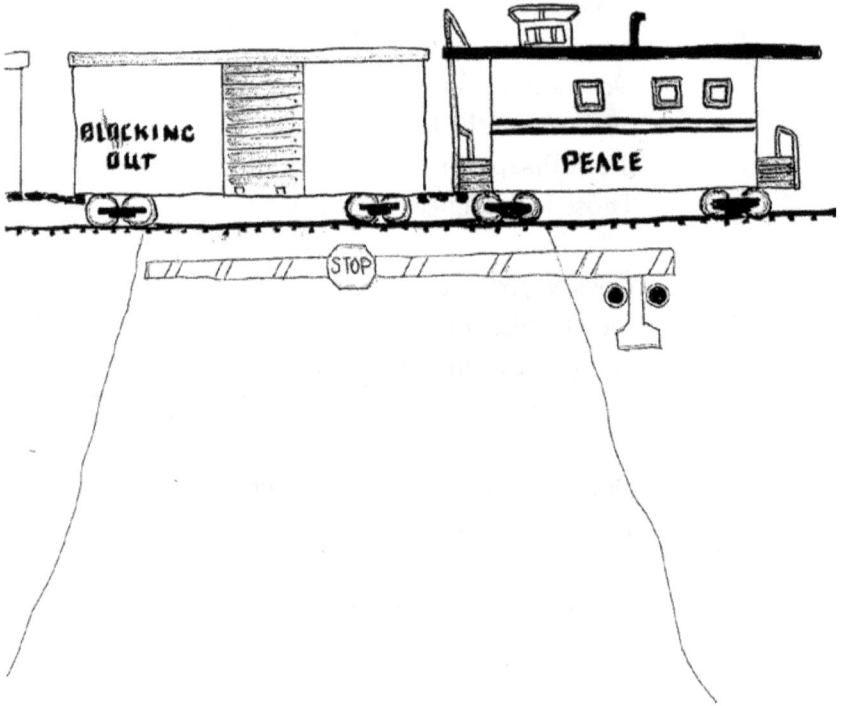

Blocking Out

Blocking Out

A train passed this morning,
each car sporting a mural
some city kid spent the night
squaring, sketching, and painting.

There's much romance in trains,
I think,
as they head somewhere
far beyond our daily scope.
I sat a mental hobo
not knowing east or west.
The train left its marks on me
like the tracks of a junkie - - - -

I imagined how that drug
would rush up my arm,
spilling long lines of rail
for a vagabond engineer
who'd have clouds for eyes
and take me out of sight
toward the heart of America.

How I felt the vibrations!
A rumbling shook my desk,
awakened that thing in me
that moved horizons.

The last car I saw was red
with large black letters
across the side that read
                    PEACE . . .
                         — 2003

185

Still Friends

Still Friends

You'd think she didn't know —
preoccupied with the hunt,
giving without saying,
head bent, eyes down
like she's the only one.
How she loved the sun, and
how she loved to play.

Colors fall black and white.
How dark winter can be.
Wondering what she thinks,
I want to ask her,
but I've learned
when to make space
and hope her pain isn't me,
as I can sometimes be a pain.
No comments please!
So in her catlike way,
she takes her space.
You cannot call a cat.
She will not appear.
You can only hope she
passes your way,
finds your lap,
purrs a little —
her way of saying,
"Still friends," and
when she gets up to go,
no boundary can
contain her.

— 2002

Sometimes the Ruler of the Pen

Sometimes the Ruler of the Pen

After all these years, I remain
a necessary friendless.
It's an empty pain that touches me —
so empty and so endless,
conditionally reclusive,
concealed by moments of fright
so that fear relays a comfort
to brood the solitary night.
Only then do thoughts have promise
that I selfishly destine to the line —
the verse I write so solemn —
ink dried, defined, its mine!

As others before me, by fate or chance,
it is our promise to defend
the choice to be the victim and,
sometimes, the ruler of the pen.

—1985

What's in a Name?

What's in a Name?

In our family, as in some,
we each have different names —
Christian names, yes, but surnames, too.
My wife and I have different names,
and our names are different from
our son's names, and our daughter's
name is different, too.

What can a name bring anyway?

My cat knew her name.
Her name was Sybil, but
we called her Giblet
or Sybilletti or The Gibster.
There were many other
foolish names, too,
When I called her those names,
she looked away in disgust,
but for food she'd come called by any name
or none at all.

She didn't put much stock in names.
Mostly, she appeared at suppertime,
sit in her chair humanlike, curl her
tail over her feet, and understood
she was very different from us.

No amount of name-calling could
tear her away from a mouse
or the skylight's sunny rays.

On the other hand, I might fall
apart with the memory of my name
shouted in my father's voice.

— 2001

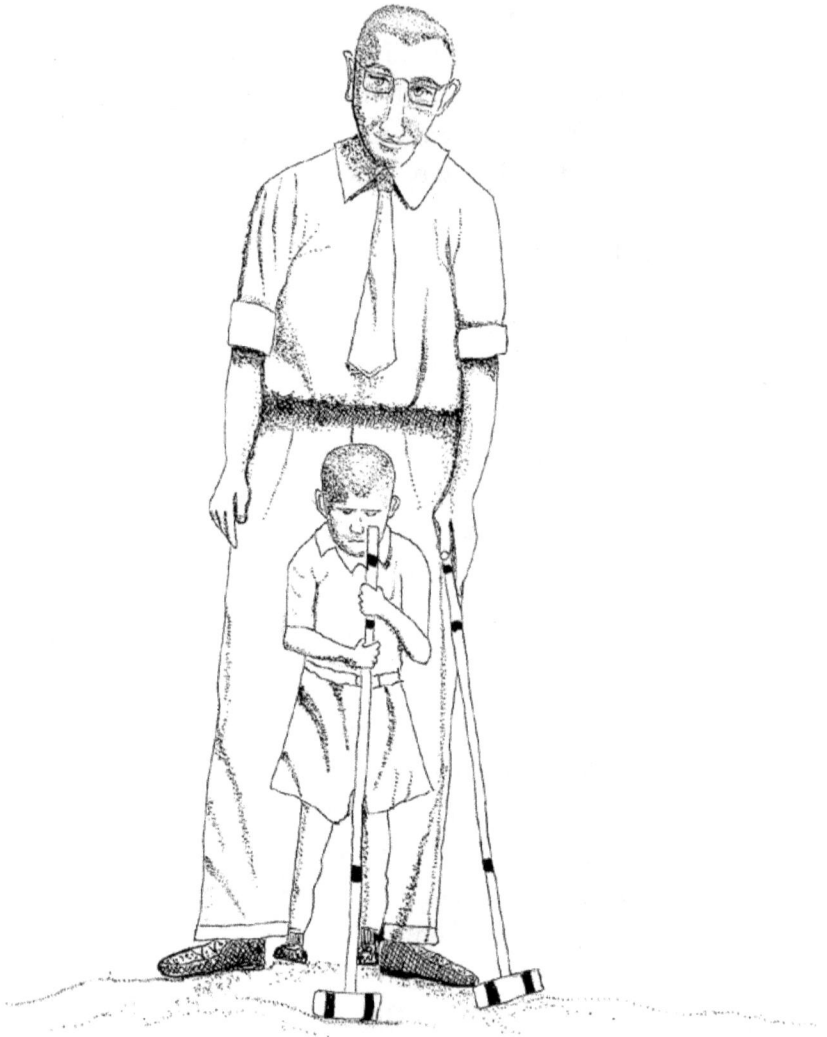

Grandpa

Grandpa

in loving memory of Joseph Fournier

Everything fades in time,
even eternal view.
When castle towers fall
our star turns deeper blue.

Beyond our inhibitions
is a place we saw in youth
a stone scattered plateau
symbolizing truth.

Perhaps an aged wisdom
suggests a silent pass
but the heart bleeds indignant
reproaching all the past.

Ask what are we here for
the answers come so late
why do we have such doubts
when Grandpa had such faith.

I hope he chased his dreams
with but few left to go
for the crimsonness of sunsets
is waking in his afterglow.

He's tested our forever
the limits ancestors call
and became the smallest block
that build the strongest wall.

He and many like him
worked hard, they didn't quit
they forged a beautiful freedom
for our children to forget.

I've seen what makes a patriot
a certain kind of brave
I hope you hear me Grandpa
thanks for all you gave.

—1980

Things Chased

Things Chased

Why does she chase the ball
yet sometimes not chase it?
Just playful at times, I guess,
or enjoys the hunt, perhaps.
Is it green to her?
Does it look round?
Can she see the rotation?
Her eyes dilate so, the ball
seems alive inside of her.

Suddenly it occurs to me—
Why do I chase the ball?

I miss her surprise attacks,
her sidewise prances,
and, you know, I was thinking,
it's really not so bad to be
a chaser of things.
Dogs retrieve.
You never see a cat retrieve.
"Things chased should never win,"
she once told me.

One night, I watched her with a mouse.
The mouse didn't move, so she
couldn't find it. By chance, if
you should come back to life as
a mouse and a cat is chasing you,
stay still—

forever!!!

—2002

Starry Night

Starry Night

Starry Night is one of my favorite paintings by Van Gogh.
"Birches" by Robert Frost contains the line, "Earth is the right place for love."

Oh, how Sybil loved it,
how he built a world:
horizon of roughed-out
boards and tarpaper.
Can't you see the doors,
windows to the universe?

She studied it that way.
Sturdy beams traced light
holding each star in place.
How clouds almost moved
and the little village so right.
"It's right for love," she told me.

Those tortoise-shell houses
beneath the cypress trees —
could it be the idea of night
lighted by a seventy-five-watt moon
tracing the furrowed lands
where Vincent once stood
and painted Sunflowers
and later, in anger, the blackest crows —

a carpenter of majesty
with a bag full of nails
hammering those paints to
build a heart from dreams.

— 2000

Snowflakes

Snowflakes

drifting together
alone to themselves
shaking their way to earth
as high as you see
but not from the sun
they appear altogether
but special each one
they sail and tumble
in gusts of wind
the clothes for a gale
or maybe it's skin
arranging themselves at
mother's command
alone they are nothing
together they stand
at a touch they will melt
in the palm of your hand
never to float
never to fly
or never to mound
up very high

                                    −1983

Paradise

Paradise

Somewhere in between
what should and should not be,
island sand so white
beneath the coconut tree.

A clock that shows no sign
of the patterns of the past,
only the sun's golden rays
til they have shown their last.

Where dreams are not betrayed
by bitterness and hate,
they grow in the form of clouds
and rain their every fate.

The only way to gauge
each perfect afternoon
is in the decision that we gave
in choosing to maroon.

—1984

Too Thin

Too Thin

The books on my shelf fell
from the ends like an
unlatched accordion.

The large volume of Shakespeare
and the Norton's remained standing
while the newer books were too thin
to keep themselves upright. I had so
many books and no means
to keep them on end,
So,

I propped the others between the Renaissance art books
and large family Bible.

Days later, the Bible moved and
the books fell again.

I wasn't sure if I had enough faith for the Bible to hold
its place, so I put it against the wall of my house and
on the other end, I stacked my *Drawing* magazines.

That made for very sturdy bookends.

Then yesterday my house
fell over . . .

                                        —1994

The Last Stop before Home

The Last Stop before Home

Trains still intrigue me—
lonesome on their way
or waiting as they do
for me to join them.
They sound different in summer
clicking around some bend.
I guess I'll be a train today
knowing where I must go,
always seeing where I've been,
just to travel the world
and never get off track.
It's a journey for questions
about the rhythm of the ties
and the smoothness of the air,
slipstreaming steel or
why the sun stings your face
as you ponder cloud shapes
and name the colors of the sky.
Why don't we have more trains,
one for each of us to take
alone for a day to a place
we've never been before.
All of it comes to me as we
pass the last stop before home.

—2009

Brian Fournier
photo © by Marcia Gagliardi

About the Poet/Artist

Brian Fournier was born in Gardner Massachusetts, and spent his early years in Athol. He went to Athol schools, graduating in 1966 from Athol High School.

He spent four years, including three overseas, in the United States Air Force as a military policeman. When discharged from the military, he attended Mount Wachusett Community College and received an associate of science degree in general studies. Later, he matriculated to Fitchburg State College and received his bachelor of arts degree in English/professional writing. He pursued a masters degree but never finished.

Brian also spent several years under the tutelage of artist Joyce Dorow learning the art of oil painting.During past thirty-five years, he's gained proficiency in several art mediums, including-pencil drawing, pastel pencils, color pencils, pen and ink, colored inks. and watercolors. He also maintains his practice of writing poems and short stories.

His award-winning poetry and art, including from Keene, New Hampshire, Art in the Park, has been published in anthologies.

In other environments, Brian worked for twenty-two years at the L. S. Starrett Company, Athol, in sales, sales engineering, and the special order department for design and build measuring instruments. He also worked in and helped develop the thread-gage order entry process.

Brian also spent sixteen years with the Rodney Hunt Company of Orange helping develop and refine the order entry process.

He applied writing-for-business skills to define product and catalog descriptions for both companies. At Starrett, he trained sales department employees in matters of product knowledge and customer service. At Rodney Hunt he trained sales engineers in the order entry process.

He lives in Orange with his wife, Marlene.

Colophon

Text, captions, and titles for *About My Cat and Other Tales* are set in the font Book Antiqua, which closely resembles Palatino and is almost indistinguishable from the original in a genre inspired by Italian traditions of handwriting and calligraphy.

www.ingramcontent.com/pod-product-compliance
Lightning Source LLC
Chambersburg PA
CBHW051955090426
42741CB00008B/1398